RESEARCH FOUNDATION REVIEW 2018

CFA Institute
Research
Foundation

Statement of Purpose

The CFA Institute Research Foundation is a not-for-profit organization established to promote the development and dissemination of relevant research for investment practitioners worldwide.

Cover credit: ithinksky / E+ / Getty Images

ISBN 978-1-944960-71-1

CONTENTS

I. THE YEAR IN REVIEW

II. MONOGRAPH SUMMARIES

III. LITERATURE REVIEW SUMMARIES

IV. BRIEFS SUMMARIES

V. MULTIMEDIA SUMMARIES

VI. WORKSHOP FOR THE PRACTITIONER SUMMARIES

VII. AWARDS AND RECOGNITION

VIII. RECENT PUBLICATIONS

I. THE YEAR IN REVIEW

DISRUPTION LOOMS LARGE: A MESSAGE FROM PAUL SMITH, CFA

Paul Smith, CFA
President and CEO
CFA Institute

Welcome to the CFA Institute Research Foundation Review 2018.

As I reflect on my five years as president and CEO of CFA Institute, I see much that we can be proud of. Over the course of our long history, we have been steadfast in our mission to lead the investment profession globally by promoting the highest standards of ethics, education, and professional excellence for the ultimate benefit of society.

Our profession has evolved greatly since our founding in 1947, but education remains a key component of our cause. Through the Research Foundation, we seek to provide independent, high-quality research that helps investment professionals effectively fulfill their duties with prudence, loyalty, and care.

The Research Foundation is only one piece of our suite of market-leading educational products, which also includes the Future of Finance, *Enterprising Investor*, and the *Financial Analysts Journal*. It is through these channels that we seek to educate and engage investment management professionals across the globe.

The passing of John Bogle in January 2019 has caused me to ponder his enormous contributions to our industry, many of which were made possible through his dedication to reason, research, and ongoing professional development. His mind did not rest easily. He pushed the industry to change, he pursued his ideas with passion, and he contributed to our industry through his scholarly ways. His research at Princeton University led him to embark on a career in investment management, and he never stopped thinking about ways in which our industry could improve. He was an academic at heart—in addition to being a visionary business leader.

For our industry to deliver on its ultimate mission, we must be aligned with our clients' interests. Jack believed, without any hesitation, that investors' interests must come first. We have espoused this view since our founding, and so we are kindred spirits with Jack and pay homage to his status as an icon in our field.

Jack was perhaps the ultimate disrupter. These days, professionals in our industry face disruption every day across myriad fronts. Disruptions loom large, forcing all of us to be forward thinking. As well-trained investment professionals, we counsel our clients to prepare for volatility and to have a long-term view. We need to be prepared for volatility within our industry as well, even if forecasting the future of our profession 10 years down the road seems nearly impossible.

We can face disruption, in part, by learning from both the successes and failings of the past. We stand 10 years removed from the global financial crisis. For some, that may seem like a lifetime ago; for others, it remains fresh in their minds. Indeed, regulators continue to promulgate rules and regulations designed to prevent a repeat of that near catastrophe. I have no doubt that the systemic failings that led to that global crisis will be researched well into the future—much in the same way that scholars continue to explore the roots of the Great Depression.

The global financial crisis proved that the world is indeed a small and interconnected place. One shock to a singular economy can cause seismic reverberations around the world. So, I am very pleased to see that the Research Foundation has broadened its offerings and has translated research pieces from many other markets. We as professionals must not be myopic in our thinking and must keep a global view.

As I prepare to retire from my role at the end of 2019, I applaud the Research Foundation for its ongoing commitment to serious research in our field. Long may it last.

MESSAGE FROM THE RESEARCH FOUNDATION CHAIR

Theodore R. Aronson, CFA
Chair
CFA Institute Research Foundation

I take the reins of the CFA Institute Research Foundation at a particularly productive period in its history.

In addition to the numerous publications discussed in these pages, the Research Foundation has produced two award-winning monographs: David Chambers and Elroy Dimson's *Financial Market History: Reflections on the Past for Investors Today* (2016) and Ronald N. Kahn's *The Future of Investment Management* (2018). (It is fun to note that both volumes reside on my bookshelf next to Roger G. Ibbotson and Rex Sinquefield's *Stocks, Bonds, Bills, and Inflation*, another Research Foundation publication from 1977—the year I earned my CFA charter!)

The trustees strive to produce the highest-quality research that is relevant to investment practitioners. Ably led by Bud Haslett, CFA, executive director; Laurence B. Siegel, director of research; and Luis Garcia-Feijóo, CFA, CIPM, assistant director of research, our organization scours the world for topics and authors to provide an important aspect of the CFA Institute mission of education and enlightenment.

After all, research is the lifeblood of what financial analysts do: Fundamental research drives security values, market research makes (some!) sense of market behavior, economic research is driven by macroeconomic forces, and quantitative research marries them all. From Ben Graham's "intrinsic value" and "margin of safety" to Robert Shiller's "irrational exuberance," to Paul Samuelson's re-introduction of the "random walk" of security prices, to Bill Sharpe's capital asset pricing model, progress advances as a result of research.

In his 2018 monograph, Kahn forecast that it is a great time for a *quantitatively* oriented 28-year-old to join our profession. I'm reminded of a wonderful statement by Robert McNamara, former secretary of defense and president of Ford Motor Company. The 1960s were a similar time of major quantitative advances, and McNamara—a quant!—nicely summarized to financial analysts the intersection of the intellectual and the practical—their toolkit of skills: "A computer does not substitute for judgment any more than a pencil substitutes for literacy. But writing without a pencil is no particular advantage."

The Research Foundation lies at the nexus of all these activities. I am honored to lead a team of volunteer trustees dedicated to our profession. On behalf of those colleagues, thank you for consuming our intellectual output and providing donations to further the cause. Every single penny supports those efforts; thus, it is fair to say that voluntary donations to the CFA Institute Research Foundation pay substantial dividends!

EXECUTIVE DIRECTOR'S REPORT

Bud Haslett, CFA
Executive Director
CFA Institute Research Foundation

Continuing its five-decade tradition of producing relevant, practitioner-focused research, the CFA Institute Research Foundation had another strong year in 2018, publishing three monographs, a literature review, and six briefs. Content topics ranged from alternative investments to sustainable investing and included such areas as risk tolerance, quantitative equity investing, high-yield securities, and popularity of investments. This year also included the superb publication of a multiyear project on the future of investment management by BlackRock's Ronald N. Kahn.

We saw a number of firsts in 2018, including the publication of a brief on the capital markets of a particular global region, in this case Latin America, edited by CFA Society Brazil president Mauro Miranda, CFA. In addition, we released our first brief compilation, "Risk Profiling and Tolerance: Insights for the Private Wealth Manager." Our compilations are a series of briefs on a particular topic that are combined into a single publication. We also began translations in Arabic and Japanese that we will complete in 2019, which will add to our already completed content translations in Chinese, French, Portuguese, and Spanish. These translations—and the growing volume of global Research Foundation content—showcase the increasingly global presence of the Research Foundation.

In another first, CFA Institute posted on its website video recordings of a conference, "2008 Financial Crisis: A 10-Year Review," organized by the Massachusetts Institute of Technology, New York University, and Annual Reviews. The event featured world-class speakers and Nobel laureates, such as Ben Bernanke, Mervyn King, Jean-Claude Trichet, Robert Merton, Myron Scholes, and Robert Engle. Spending some time viewing these videos, available for free, is an investment worth making.

Once again in 2018, the Research Foundation had the honor of working with almost 100 member societies around the globe. This work included providing complimentary speakers for more than 45 society events and providing more than 30,000 complimentary Research Foundation books to societies and others to distribute at their events. We also published research from the Latin American member societies, CFA Society New York, and CFA Society Boston and will soon be publishing content from CFA Society France and the Louis Bachelier Group. Additionally, we began a new program to assist "pre-societies" as they build up the critical mass needed to become full-fledged societies, sending Research Foundation books and other materials to the groups so they can distribute them at events and during company and government outreach efforts.

The winners of the seventh annual Research Foundation Society Awards included CFA Society Switzerland, for its work with the sustainable investing monograph; CFA Society Brazil, for its work on various events and activities using Research Foundation publications; and CFA Society New York, for its innovative design of a Research Foundation–based webpage on its website. We look forward to working with other societies as we prepare to present the eighth annual Research Foundation Society Awards in 2019.

Esteemed speakers at the 17th Research Foundation Workshop for the Practitioner, held in Hong Kong in May 2018, included Joanne M. Hill discussing her book *A Comprehensive Guide to Exchange-Traded Funds (ETFs)*, which was recently translated into Chinese. The workshop also featured Donald R. Chambers and Keith H. Black of the Chartered Alternative Investment Analyst (CAIA) Association, discussing their book *Alternative Investments: A Primer for Investment Professionals*. The sessions were moderated by the Research Foundation's Joachim Klement, CFA, and all three speakers graciously agreed to conduct multistop speaking tours in Asia following the workshop.

The Research Foundation extends congratulations to William N. Goetzmann, the Edwin J. Beinecke Professor of Finance and Management Studies and director of the International Center for Finance at the Yale School of Management, for winning the 2018 James R. Vertin Award. This award, presented in China for the first time, recognizes individuals who have produced a body of research notable for its relevance and enduring value to investment professionals. The award was established in 1996 to honor James R. Vertin, CFA, for his outstanding leadership in promoting excellence and relevance in research and education. This year's award was particularly significant because Mr. Vertin passed away in 2018.

During 2018, the Research Foundation transferred all of its online content to a new hosting platform and the online presence was totally revamped. We are working on optimizing the many changes that occurred; when complete, they will lead to a much more efficient searching and viewing experience. In 2018, we also experienced our first full year of operating as a part of the research group at CFA Institute, which includes the *Financial Analysts Journal*, the Future of Finance, and now *Enterprising Investor*. Combining our strengths across the research group of CFA Institute provides the Research Foundation with ever-greater opportunities for impact.

Research Foundation material will return to the CFA Program exam curriculum in the near future, as commitments are in place to use content from the Research Foundation monographs on ETFs and trading for the upcoming readings. Many thanks to Barbara Petitt, CFA, and the curriculum staff for the great work they have done and are doing with the CFA Program exam readings.

As usual, I would like to thank the dozens and dozens of individuals directly responsible for the Research Foundation, including CFA Institute staff and leadership, as well as the many Board of Trustees members responsible for directing the strategic path of the Research Foundation. Thanks, too, to our research director, Laurence B. Siegel; our new associate research director, Luis Garcia-Feijóo, CFA, CIPM; and our project manager, Jessica Lawson, for their tremendous contributions to the operation of the Research Foundation. Hats off as well to our authors, who create the excellent content that we publish, as well as to CFA Institute for its financial support and to the more than 10,000 donating members who make the Research Foundation financially viable. As I begin my ninth year as executive director of the Research Foundation, I am truly honored to be a part of this wonderful organization and look forward to more years of guiding it along the path of continued success.

RESEARCH DIRECTOR'S REPORT

Laurence B. Siegel
Gary P. Brinson Director of Research
CFA Institute Research Foundation

In 2018, the CFA Institute Research Foundation published three research monographs, a literature review, and six briefs. We also posted video of an exceptional conference, "2008 Financial Crisis: A 10-Year Review," on our website.

Research Monographs

Research monographs are books intended to have a long shelf life. In chronological order, the monographs we published in 2018 are

- *Alternative Investments: A Primer for Investment Professionals*, by Donald R. Chambers, CAIA, Keith Black, CFA, CAIA, and Nelson J. Lacey, CFA;
- *The Future of Investment Management*, by Ronald N. Kahn; and
- *Popularity: A Bridge between Classical and Behavioral Finance*, by Roger G. Ibbotson, Thomas M. Idzorek, CFA, Paul D. Kaplan, CFA, and James X. Xiong, CFA.

Donald R. Chambers, CAIA, Keith Black, CFA, CAIA, and Nelson J. Lacey, CFA, *Alternative Investments: A Primer for Investment Professionals*

In a collaborative effort with the Chartered Alternative Investment Analyst (CAIA) Association, the authors translate the often-baffling jargon associated with alternative investing into plain English. They define alternatives expansively as any asset or asset pool that is not a long-only, unleveraged position in equities or investment-grade bonds. Thus, alternatives can include unconventional strategies or structures as well as nontraditional underlying sources of return.

The need for a thorough primer on this topic has existed for a long time. Although traditional asset managers are sometimes prolific writers, alternative asset managers tend not to be (they are often traders or entrepreneurs and not the most contemplative sort), so the literature on alternatives is quite limited and this volume is a welcome addition to it.

Chambers, Black, and Lacey describe the strategies used by, and risks associated with, each major category of alternatives: hedge funds, private equity, infrastructure funds, real estate and other real assets, commodities, and derivatives and structured products. Although the monograph is called a primer, the authors' treatment is quite advanced and encyclopedic.

The authors also look at process issues, including due diligence, performance measurement and evaluation, and the special challenges involved in benchmarking these assets (which often do not have usable benchmarks). They conclude by summarizing the case for alternative investing, which, in their view, is supported by the high valuations of traditional assets, the need to move the efficient frontier outward by expanding beta exposures beyond the traditional stock and bond categories, and the ability to add alpha through investment skill.

Ronald N. Kahn, *The Future of Investment Management*

Ronald N. Kahn is one of the most respected investment managers in the industry and one of its most eloquent writers. In *The Future of Investment Management*, Kahn combines work he has delivered in lectures and published articles with a great deal of new material. Following the "rule of sevens," which says that good things come in sevens (or fives or threes—no even numbers), Kahn presents seven insights into active management and seven trends in investment management. The seven trends are (1) active to passive, (2) increased competition, (3) changing market environments, (4) big data, (5) smart beta, (6) investing beyond returns (investing to achieve goals other than maximum return per unit of risk taken, for example, in environmental, social, and governance strategies), and (7) fee compression.

But first, in what will for many readers be the most elucidating part of the book, Kahn recounts the intellectual history of the investment management profession from the viewpoint of someone who participated in creating that history. As co-author (with Richard C. Grinold) of the groundbreaking book *Active Portfolio Management: A Quantitative Approach for Producing Superior Returns and Controlling Risk* (first published in 1994), Kahn applied the quantitative techniques pioneered by Harry Markowitz, William Sharpe, and Barr Rosenberg to the practical problems of constructing portfolios. He brings this history to life by showing how the ideas of the investment pioneers of the 1950s, 1960s, and 1970s are affecting the lives of ordinary people in a different century (e.g., through index funds, factor or "smart beta" funds, and a sophisticated and accurate system of performance measurement).

The future of investment management will involve less picking of low-hanging fruit, more effort, and possibly less personal reward. But investing will continue to be one of the most intellectually stimulating as well as economically rewarding fields of endeavor. Lest anyone be discouraged, Kahn writes that "today may not be a great time to be a 50-year-old investment manager, but . . . it is a great time to be a quantitatively oriented 28-year-old entering the field."

Roger G. Ibbotson, Thomas M. Idzorek, CFA, Paul D. Kaplan, CFA, and James X. Xiong, CFA, *Popularity: A Bridge between Classical and Behavioral Finance*

In the 1970s, Roger G. Ibbotson, with co-author Rex Sinquefield, was the first to document the historical returns on a variety of different asset classes ("stocks, bonds, bills, and inflation"). Ibbotson and Sinquefield identified the return differences as risk premiums earned by investors for taking the risk of one asset class (say, stocks) compared with another (say, bonds).

In the next decade, Ibbotson, with Jeffrey Diermeier, CFA (a former CFA Institute president and CEO) and Laurence B. Siegel, conceived of—but didn't formalize—a "new equilibrium theory" that links the returns on assets to *all* of their characteristics, not just risk. These characteristics include taxability, liquidity, and other attributes that any investor might like or dislike and that different investors like or dislike to different degrees.

The result of all this heterogeneity is that, unlike in the capital asset pricing model (CAPM), it is rational for different investors to hold different risky-asset portfolios—not just portfolios with different betas (positions on the capital market line) but portfolios with different underlying components. For example, someone with a long time horizon might load up on illiquid stocks, expecting to earn a higher return because other investors, needing liquidity, shun those issues.

In their 2018 monograph, *Popularity*, Ibbotson, Idzorek, Kaplan, and Xiong, all from Ibbotson Associates and its parent company, Morningstar, turn this set of observations into a proper theory. They note that there are "many premiums [in the market] that may or may not be related to risk, but all are related to investing in something that is unpopular in some way." They consider premiums to be the result of characteristics that are systematically *unpopular*; that is, popularity makes the price of a security higher and the expected return lower, all other things being equal. This principle can be used to structure actively managed portfolios that fit a particular investor's preferences for, or aversions to, specific characteristics.

The authors do the math. They set forth a formal popularity asset pricing model and conduct a variety of empirical tests, finding that such factors as "moats" and "brand" can be priced just as size and value can be priced.

Popularity constructs a bridge between classical and behavioral finance because the effects the authors observe can exist whether investors are rational or irrational. For example, a rational investor might want more liquidity than his neighbor and pay extra (sacrificing return) for a security offering that liquidity. But an investor can also be irrational, exhibiting behavioral biases and making cognitive errors. The popularity framework embraces both possibilities regarding investor rationality and is thus a more complete framework for understanding asset pricing than either pure rationality or a purely behavioral approach.

Literature Review

Ying L. Becker and Marc R. Reinganum, *The Current State of Quantitative Equity Investing*

In their incisive literature review, Professor Ying L. Becker of Suffolk University and factor investing pioneer Marc R. Reinganum (who co-discovered the small stock effect more than 40 years ago) assess the state of "quant" equity investing. They focus on factors but start with a primer on risk and return, modern portfolio theory, and the classic theories of asset pricing that prefigured the later discovery of common factors (other than the market factor) in stock returns.

The age of factor investing began in the 1970s with Barr Rosenberg's discovery of "extra-market covariance" (exceptions to the single-factor model of William Sharpe, which says that stock returns are correlated only with the overall market) and with Stephen A. Ross and Richard Roll's multifactor arbitrage pricing theory. But it was Reinganum himself, along with Rolf Banz, who identified the first simple, usable factor: small size. Small-cap stocks had outperformed their large-cap brethren by a wide margin at the time Reinganum and Banz did their research and have continued to perform differently from (but not always better than) large-cap stocks.

Rosenberg's discovery set off a race to find other factors, which are now the basis for a blizzard of investment products, such as factor-based exchange-traded funds and mutual funds. Becker and Reinganum's literature review recounts the race to find and exploit as many factors as possible, a "zoo" of factors according to American Finance Association president John H. Cochrane, who is skeptical that all of them exist.

Becker and Reinganum then turn their attention to big data and dynamic factor modeling (factor timing), which are the latest wave of quantitative techniques in equity management. Although "quant" investing received some bad press a few years ago because of the poor performance of some popular models, the authors conclude that "quantitative equity management is alive and well—and intellectually active—as investors seek to better manage risk and return." Actually, it is hard to think of a well-managed investment effort as being anything other than quantitative, or at least analytically rigorous.

Research Foundation Briefs

Elke U. Weber and Joachim Klement, CFA, "Risk Tolerance and Circumstances"

In this contribution to the already rich literature on assessing individual investors' behavior toward risk, Elke U. Weber and former Research Foundation board chair Joachim Klement, CFA, distinguish between various uses of the term "risk tolerance." Risk tolerance can be an underlying and stable characteristic of an individual, or it can be an attribute that changes with circumstances, such as wealth, age, and market conditions. The authors review a number of studies, showing, for example, that investors' risk tolerance declined during the crisis of 2008, that it declines with age, and that it is lower for women than for men. Advisers and their clients can benefit from knowledge of the research on these fine points of risk assessment. The authors' advice to financial advisers: "Be aware . . . educate . . . nudge . . . hold hands."

Edited by Joachim Klement, CFA, "Risk Profiling and Tolerance: Insights for the Private Wealth Manager"

With the publication of the "Risk Tolerance and Circumstances" brief, the five-part series on risk profiling and risk tolerance was complete, so the Research Foundation combined all the articles in the series, added a new foreword and preface, and published "Risk Profiling and Tolerance: Insights for the Private Wealth Manager." This compilation brief, edited by Joachim Klement, CFA, includes the following components:

- Foreword by Bob Dannhauser, CFA;
- "Preface: Investing Is Rational, Money Is Emotional," by Joachim Klement, CFA;
- "Investor Risk Profiling: An Overview," by Joachim Klement, CFA;
- "Risk Profiling through a Behavioral Finance Lens," by Michael Pompian, CFA;
- "Financial Risk Tolerance: A Psychometric Review," by John E. Grable;
- "Risk Tolerance and Circumstances," by Elke U. Weber and Joachim Klement, CFA; and
- "New Vistas in Risk Profiling," by Greg B. Davies.

Edited by Mauro Miranda, CFA, "Latin American Local Capital Markets: Challenges and Solutions"

In a compilation edited by the Research Foundation trustee Mauro Miranda, CFA, a group of authors from seven Latin American countries—Argentina, Brazil, Chile, Colombia, Mexico, Peru, and Uruguay—describes the financial system, market structure, and access to capital in those countries.

The critical event in recent Argentine history is its emergence from sovereign debt default in 2016, once again attracting foreign investors to the country's local markets. Once-fast-growing Brazil, now recovering from a severe recession, faces such challenges as "the crowding out of private capital markets by public issuance." Chile, which is quite prosperous, is analyzed from the perspective of the country's fixed-income market and its domination by pension funds, which are long-term investors, resulting in little trading or foreign investment. Colombia is becoming a successful emerging economy, but its capital markets—especially its equity market—are underdeveloped. Mexico has recently experienced a period of relatively strong growth, but "the key to capital market development . . . seems to lie with the expansion of credit." Peru suffers from "the absence of a financial culture," so liquidity and market depth are thin; there are few equities. Uruguay is small and has less well-developed capital markets than its neighbors but is prosperous and offers a stable environment for business.

Edited by Martin Fridson, CFA, "Foundations of High-Yield Analysis"

Edited by Martin Fridson, CFA, one of the best-known and most widely published analysts of the high-yield bond markets, this brief consists of six essays relating to the market for below-investment-grade bonds. The first essay, by Fridson himself, is titled "Understanding Default Rates, Recoveries, Spreads, and Returns." Fridson summarizes his views as follows: "You should be skeptical of even widely accepted methods of analyzing and forecasting the performance of high-yield bonds. . . . You should [also] be cautious in applying traditional fixed-income analytical techniques to high-yield bonds."

Bill Hoffmann's "The Art of High-Yield Credit Analysis" is a case study that analyzes Kraton Performance Polymers' acquisition of Arizona Chemical in 2015, using substantial leverage (debt). Studying a long historical period, Diane Vazza's "Forecasting the High-Yield Default Rate" shows how default rates on high-yield bonds are affected by macroeconomic factors and market cycles. In "Corporate Bankruptcy: Primer on Process and Prospects," Anders Maxwell shows how "bankruptcy reorganizations—and related out-of-court restructurings—represent an opportunistic niche in high-yield credit markets." Taking advantage of such special situations requires a keen understanding of law as well as finance. Maxwell counsels that studying corporate failure may be more revealing than studying corporate success.

In "An Introduction to High-Yield Bond Covenants," Saish Setty provides a primer on debt covenants, which are a key element of the indentures (legal contracts) that underlie bond issuances. Covenants may be affirmative (requiring the borrower to do something) or negative (prohibiting the borrower from doing something). Readers also find out what a hookie dook is.

Finally, the late Michael F. Brown, in "Dynamics of the High-Yield Bond Market," introduces the reader to some of the more advanced math governing the bond market and high-yield bonds in particular.

Edited by Michael J. Greis, CFA, "Mainstreaming Sustainable Investing"

This brief presents the contents of the 2016 Sustainable Investing Seminar; the seminars have been run annually by CFA Society Boston since 2013. The editor, Michael J. Greis, defines sustainable investing in terms of the 1987 Brundtland Commission report to the United Nations: "Sustainable development is development that meets the needs of the present without compromising the ability of future generations to meet their own needs." This broad concept applies to investing through techniques now usually known as ESG (environmental, social, and governance) investing.

In addition to Greis's introduction, the brief consists of write-ups of the four presentations at the seminar:

- "Investing in an Era of Disruption and Transformational Change: The Value of Material ESG Information," by George Serafeim, Harvard Business School;
- "Machine Learning and Big Data Enable a Quantitative Approach to ESG Investing," by Andreas Feiner, Arabesque Asset Management;

- "Analyzing the Performance of ESG Factors in a Mixed Asset Setting," by Andreas Hoepner, University College Dublin; and
- "Understanding and Capitalizing on Systemic Impacts of ESG Factors," by Steve Lydenberg, Domini Social Investments.

The unifying theme of the presentations is that, in social investing pioneer Erika Karp's words, "sustainable investing is just investing." In other words, the analytic tools and intellectual framework used to make any active management decision can and should be applied to investing for environmental and social goals.

Momtchil Pojarliev, CFA, "Some Like It Hedged"

In this research brief on currency hedging, currency manager Momtchil Pojarliev, CFA, notes that most currency exposure taken by investors is inadvertent: They don't do it to make money; rather, it is a side effect of investing in securities issued outside one's home country. Asking whether investors should hedge (and how much), Pojarliev finds that "investors whose base currency is negatively correlated with global equities, such as the US dollar and the Japanese yen, will reduce the volatility of their portfolios by fully hedging foreign currency exposure." However, investors whose base currency is positively correlated with global equities should hedge less or not at all and may benefit from exposure to the US dollar. The author also notes that hedging is costly and must be evaluated as to whether it is worth the expense. This work builds on the renowned currency-hedging study by Fischer Black in the *Financial Analysts Journal* in 1989 ("Universal Hedging: Optimizing Currency Risk and Reward in International Equity Portfolios") and on the author's own 2012 research monograph (with co-author Richard Levich), *A New Look at Currency Investing.*

Future Work

In 2019, the Research Foundation will offer monographs on restoring the growth of economic productivity (a collection of works by prominent economists), structuring the responsibilities of fund fiduciaries for optimum performance, investing for a secure retirement, and assessing whether there is a systemic retirement crisis. We will also release briefs and a literature review as they are produced, and we look forward to an exciting year.

II. MONOGRAPH SUMMARIES

ALTERNATIVE INVESTMENTS: A PRIMER FOR INVESTMENT PROFESSIONALS

by Donald R. Chambers, CAIA, Keith Black, CFA, CAIA, and Nelson J. Lacey

Alternative Investments: A Primer for Investment Trustees provides an overview of alternative investing for investment trustees and others with substantial experience regarding traditional investments in stocks and bonds but limited experience regarding alternative investments. It begins by exploring the differences between institutional-quality alternative investments and traditional investments, going beyond the common approach of describing assets to an intuitive approach that describes their intrinsic differences. Alternative investments are placed in their long-term historical context, with a focus on their crucial distinguishing features—features that require management methods that differ markedly from traditional methods.

Two "pillars of portfolio oversight" are the foundation of successful asset selection and allocation in alternative investing: empirical analysis and economics reasoning. Because alternative investing uses empirical and theoretical models that are only lightly covered in traditional investing (i.e., multifactor models, statistical analysis based on higher moments), this primer focuses on the extra knowledge required by portfolio overseers who are new to such investments. For example, Chapter 2 reviews terms commonly used in alternative investing but less commonly used in traditional investing (i.e., prime brokers, private placement memoranda, and undertakings for collective investment in transferable securities, or UCITS).

Nine of the primer's 17 chapters cover the four major institutional-quality alternative investment categories: hedge funds, real assets, private equity, and structured products/derivatives.

Chapter 3 introduces hedge funds by reviewing the rationale for incorporating hedge funds in a portfolio, including their risks and potential sources of return. An asset's source of return is an explanation of why the investment might be able to generate enhanced expected returns.

Hedge fund liquidity ranges from liquid alternatives (US Investment Companies Act of 1940 funds) to limited partnerships with restrictions on redemptions and potential lock-up periods. The primer's introduction to hedge funds includes an overview of the management fees, incentive fees, hurdle rates, and high-water marks commonly found in private hedge funds. Particular attention is given to the call option–like nature of hedge fund incentive fees and the accompanying issue of moral hazard. The chapter concludes with a discussion of co-investment to mitigate conflicts of interest and a general discussion of hedge fund governance.

Chapters 4 and 5 describe various hedge fund strategies and approaches to accessing those strategies. The categories of strategies covered include macro and managed futures funds, event-driven hedge funds, relative-value funds, and equity hedge funds, with numerous examples of each. For example, Chapter 4's coverage of event-driven hedge funds includes descriptions of the following fund strategies: merger arbitrage, activists, distressed, and event-driven multistrategy. Key questions addressed in the primer regarding how an institution should *access* alternatives include the following:

- How many underlying funds provide optimal diversification?
- Should the institution use a direct investment program or pooled approaches?
- What are the relative merits of multistrategy funds, funds of funds, and fund indexes?

The approaches are not merely described; they are assessed with regard to their effect on due diligence requirements and total fees.

Chapters 6, 7, and 8 focus on real assets and the key information that portfolio overseers should possess, such as illiquidity, valuation issues, the smoothing of reported returns, potential benefits of including real assets (e.g., sources of return, diversification), challenges with using internal rate of return, and methods of access. The primer provides clear reasoning for such propositions as intellectual property being a real asset. Although some of the literature does not recognize intellectual property as a real asset, the primer clarifies the distinction between real assets and tangible assets, explaining that tangible assets have physical form, while real assets are *direct* claims on resources. The counterpart to tangible assets is intangible assets; the counterpart to real assets is financial assets (which are indirect claims on resources). For example, although intellectual property is intangible, it is clearly a direct claim on resources. Understanding of this issue is critical because intellectual property as an asset class is soaring in economic importance. As cited in the primer's first chapter, tangible assets such as land and gold dominated the world's wealth in previous centuries. In the last 100 years, however, it is intangible wealth that has fueled explosive economic growth. The assets of many of the world's largest firms (e.g., Facebook) are now composed almost entirely of intellectual property.

Private equity (including private debt) is a major segment of institutional-quality alternative investing and is addressed in Chapter 9. The chapter includes a discussion of the wide variety of types of private equity as well as access to private equity, the associated fees, the challenges of using and interpreting the internal rate of returns, the J-curve of private equity returns, and potential sources of returns.

Financial derivatives and structured products are each covered in separate chapters (Chapters 10 and 11, respectively). The chapter on financial derivatives focuses on understanding the risks from a top-level perspective. This view includes a focus on the "Greeks" (e.g., delta, gamma) and the motivations for using options, futures, forwards, and swaps. The chapter on structured products focuses on the intuition and mechanics of collateralized debt obligations (CDOs), including discussions of tranching, cash-flow waterfalls, and the various types of CDOs.

Having introduced alternatives and covered the four major asset groups in the first 11 chapters, the primer, in its remaining chapters, primarily provides portfolio-related perspectives. Chapter 12 discusses tail risk and summarizes lessons to be learned from past fund failures, including flawed investment strategies, investment strategy drift, rogue traders, operations errors, and fraud. Appropriately, the next chapter discusses due diligence, that is, the ongoing duty of investment professionals to exercise care in avoiding harm to their clients. The due diligence discussion focuses on two aspects: (1) the decision of whether to perform various aspects of due diligence internally or through outsourcing, and (2) the particular issues regarding due diligence that have been identified as being especially problematic in the area of alternative investments. The key issues include (1) four important trends in due diligence, (2) three warning signals, and (3) five issues regarding compliance programs and the Code of Ethics (which all advisers registered with the US SEC are required to adopt).

Chapters 14 and 15 turn to a discussion of returns, risk, benchmarking, return expectations, and performance attribution, focusing on those issues that are particularly important in alternative investments and relevant to asset overseers, and that tend to be relatively unfamiliar to professionals whose experience has been centered on traditional investments. For example, the first of the two chapters emphasizes the asymmetrical return distributions of many alternative investments and the potential errors from viewing returns as being roughly normally distributed. The primer provides an overview of the challenges of measuring and managing risks, including the potential for managers to "game" naive monitoring methods. Chapter 15 clarifies the often-misinterpreted concepts of alpha and beta as applied within alternative investing, and the crucial concepts of absolute and relative performance. The chapter also discusses benchmarks and asset pricing models, not in terms of their mathematical nuances but rather in terms of their usefulness in guiding how asset allocators develop realistic and logical understandings of return expectations for individual assets and portfolios.

The primer's final two chapters conclude with discussions of portfolio construction approaches (e.g., risk budgeting, risk parity) and the case for investing in alternatives (including the endowment model). The discussion highlights asset allocation as the primary determinant of portfolio returns. Thoughtful and effective asset allocation is inextricably linked to concepts such as diversification, alpha versus beta, and sources of return.

The key to the usefulness of these final chapters—as well as to the value of the primer as a whole—is the primer's focus on the most important terms and concepts. These key terms and concepts are clearly presented to the primer's intended audience: investment trustees seeking to extend their investment knowledge into the area of alternative assets and strategies.

The publication can be found at

https://www.cfainstitute.org/en/research/foundation/2018/alternative-investments-a-primer-for-investment-professionals

Use your mobile device to scan the QR code to go straight to the webpage.

THE FUTURE OF INVESTMENT MANAGEMENT

by Ronald N. Kahn

Investment management is in flux, arguably more than it has been in a long time. Active management is under pressure, with investors switching from active to index funds. New "smart beta" products offer low-cost exposures to many active ideas. Exchange-traded funds are proliferating. Markets and regulations have changed significantly over the past 10–20 years, and data and technology—which are increasingly important for investment management—are evolving even more rapidly.

In the midst of this change, what can we say about the future of investment management? What ideas will influence its evolution? What types of products will flourish over the next 5–10 years?

I use a long perspective to address these questions. I analyze the modern intellectual history of investment management—roughly, the set of ideas, developed over the past 100 years, that have influenced investment management up to now. For additional context and to understand the full arc of history, I briefly discuss the early roots of the field. As I discuss this history, I review the various ideas and insights that ultimately coalesce into a coherent understanding of investing, in spite of its uncertain nature.

One central theme that emerges is that investment management is becoming increasingly systematic. Over time, our understanding of risk has evolved from a general aversion to losing money to a precisely defined statistic we can measure and forecast. Our understanding of expected returns has evolved as the necessary data have become more available, as our understanding of fundamental value has developed, and as we have slowly come to understand the connection between return and risk and the relevance of human behavior to both. Data and technology have advanced in parallel to facilitate implementing better approaches.

Our systems of understanding this intrinsically uncertain activity of investing continue to expand, affecting the investment products we see today and those we expect to see in the future. It is as hard to imagine index funds and exchange-traded funds dominating the investment markets of the Netherlands in the 1700s as it is to imagine their absence in the global investment markets of 2018.

With an understanding of the ideas underlying investment management today, including several insights into active management, I discuss the many trends currently roiling the field. These trends, applied to the current state of investment management, suggest that investment management will evolve into three distinct branches—indexing, smart beta/factor investing, and *pure alpha* investing, where "pure alpha" refers to active returns above and beyond those arising from static exposures to smart beta factors. Each branch will offer two styles of products: those that focus exclusively on returns and those that include goals beyond returns.

The following is a chapter-by-chapter summary of the book. Chapter 1 provides an overview and introduction. Chapter 2, on the early roots of investment management, briefly defines investment management and discusses its development. What is investment management, what are its required elements, and when did those elements first appear? Investment management may go back to ancient times, but its clear historical record begins in the Netherlands in the late 1700s. Those early records show that investors already appreciated diversification and thought about value investing.

Chapter 3, on the modern history of investment management, traces the evolution of ideas and practices that have influenced the field up through today. The first efforts at developing systematic approaches began almost a century ago, partly in response to periods of wild speculation and losses like the market crash of 1929. Our understanding of investment value developed around this time, and our modern understanding of risk and portfolio construction began in the 1950s. Chapter 3 also traces the development of ideas underlying index funds—initially conceived in academia in the 1960s—and, in response, the eventual development of systematic approaches to active management.

Chapter 4, on seven insights into active management, describes key concepts required to understand efforts to outperform. This chapter begins with the "arithmetic of active management," the idea that active management is worse than a zero-sum game—that the average active manager will underperform. It then shows that the information ratio—the amount of outperformance per unit of risk—determines an active manager's ability to add value for investors. It also determines how investors should allocate risk and capital to different active products. The chapter discusses the fundamental law of active management, which breaks down the information ratio into constituent parts: skill, diversification, and efficiency. This relationship can help active managers develop new strategies and provide some guidance to investors looking to choose active managers. Other insights cover the process of forecasting returns, challenges to testing new investment ideas, and understanding how portfolio constraints affect the efficiency of implementing investment ideas.

Chapter 5, on seven trends in investment management, turns the spotlight on current directions that will influence the future of the field. These trajectories include the shift in assets from active to passive investing, the increase in competition among active managers, the changing market environment, the emergence of big data, the development of smart beta, the increased interest in what I call *investing beyond returns*—that is, investing for non-return objectives, such as environmental, social, and governance goals, as well as to earn returns—and, finally, fee compression.

Chapter 6, on the future of investment management, applies these trends to the current state of investment management—theory and practice—to forecast how the field will evolve over the next 5–10 years. As noted previously, I expect investment management to evolve into three distinct branches, with each offering two styles of products.

The investment case for indexing is compelling. Successful indexing is all about delivering exposures as cheaply and reliably as possible. The ability to provide exposures cheaply requires scale, and indexing is already dominated by a few very large firms. Although things could always go wrong in investment management, nothing would systemically threaten indexing as an investment category.

The investment case for smart beta/factor investing is fairly strong, if not as strong as the case for indexing. Like indexing, these products attempt to deliver exposures as cheaply as possible. I expect consolidation over time. A small number of firms will manage most of the smart beta/factor assets. Several things could threaten this branch of investment management: poor performance over an extended period, severe poor performance over a short period due to large and correlated outflows, and a lack of investor understanding of expected dispersion across different smart beta/factor funds.

Pure alpha investing faces the most difficult investment case—I expect the average pure alpha investor to underperform—though there are reasons to believe that some pure alpha investors can succeed. Pure alpha investing is distinctly not about delivering exposure cheaply. Instead, it involves narrow and transient ideas that require constant innovation to replace old ideas the market comes to understand. Pure alpha is capacity constrained and expensive. The most successful pure alpha firms will be research-driven boutiques, possibly including boutiques within large asset management firms. Although plenty can go wrong with individual pure alpha products, I do not see systemic threats to this branch of investing.

To add an optimistic spin on the current level of disruption in investment management, which is unsettling for many people in the field, I believe that disruption can create great opportunities. The shifting boundaries between active and passive and dramatic changes in technology augur well for new types of products and new sources of information to help managers outperform. Today may not be a great time to be a 50-year-old investment manager, but as I often tell students and colleagues studying for the CFA® Program exams, it is a great time to be a quantitatively oriented 28-year-old entering the field.

The publication can be found at
https://www.cfainstitute.org/en/research/foundation/2018/future-of-investment-management

Use your mobile device to scan the QR code to go straight to the webpage.

POPULARITY: A BRIDGE BETWEEN CLASSICAL AND BEHAVIORAL FINANCE

by Roger G. Ibbotson, Thomas M. Idzorek, CFA, Paul D. Kaplan, CFA, and James X. Xiong, CFA

Popularity is a word that embraces how much anything is liked, recognized, or desired. Popularity drives demand. In this book, we apply this concept to assets and securities to explain the premiums and so-called anomalies in security markets, especially the stock market.

Most assets and securities have a relatively fixed supply over the short or intermediate term. Popularity represents the demand for a security—or perhaps the set of reasons why a security is demanded to the extent that it is—and thus is an important determinant of prices for a given set of expected cash flows.

A common belief in the finance literature is that premiums in the market are payoffs for the *risk* of securities—that is, they are "risk" premiums. In classical finance, investors are risk averse, and market frictions are usually assumed away. In the broadest context, risk is unpopular. The largest risk premium is the equity risk premium (i.e., the extra expected return for investing in equities rather than bonds or risk-free assets). Other risk premiums include, for example, the interest rate term premium (because of the greater risk of longer-term bonds) and the default risk premium in bond markets.

There are many premiums in the market that may or may not be related to risk, but all are related to investing in something that is unpopular in some way. We consider premiums to be the result of characteristics that are systematically *unpopular*—that is, popularity makes the price of a security higher and the expected return lower, all other things being equal. Preferences that influence relative popularity can and do change over time. These premiums include the size premium, the value premium, the liquidity premium, the severe downside premium, low volatility and low beta premiums, ESG premiums and discounts, competitive advantage, brand, and reputation. In general, any type of security with characteristics that tend to be overlooked or unwanted can have a premium.

The title of this book refers to a bridge between classical and behavioral finance. Both approaches to finance rest on investor preferences, which we cast as popularity.

In classical finance, risk (and in particular, systematic risk) is the primary asset characteristic to which investors are averse. The CAPM says that all assets are priced according to a single, systematic factor—namely, "market risk" or covariance with the capitalization-weighted market portfolio. In contrast, we believe that risks can also be multi-dimensional, including various types of stock or bond risks. The specific structure of risk and different types of risk can also be priced, such as catastrophic risk. Although classical finance usually assumes away market frictions, rational investors may have preferences for market liquidity, favorable tax treatments, or asset divisibility, making assets more or less valuable to the extent they embody these characteristics.

In behavioral finance, investors may not be completely rational. Thus, investors may have preferences that go beyond rational behavior. We classify behavioral biases into two distinct types, psychological and cognitive. Psychological desires cause some assets to be more popular than others, relative to their expected cash flow and relative to other rational characteristics, such as liquidity. Investors' rationality is also limited because they make cognitive errors.

Neoclassical economics provides the rationality framework for efficient capital markets. Behavioral economics assumes limited or "bounded" rationality and thus provides the framework for prospect theory, loss aversion, framing, mental accounting, overconfidence, and other inconsistencies with rational behavior. Popularity represents all of our preferences, which can be rational or irrational, providing a bridge between classical and behavioral finance.

The CAPM is an elegant and easy-to-use theory for describing investor expected returns in an equilibrium setting. It assumes that investors are rational and risk averse. Because they can diversify away from all non-market risk, only systematic market risk in securities is priced. Securities with higher systematic risk have lower relative prices and thus higher expected returns. We introduce a new formal asset pricing model, the popularity asset pricing model (PAPM), that extends the CAPM to include all types of preferences.

The PAPM is an outgrowth of New Equilibrium Theory (NET), a framework proposed by Ibbotson, Diermeier, and Siegel (*Financial Analysts Journal* 1984) in which investors are rational but have preferences for or aversions to various security characteristics beyond the single market risk of the CAPM. Additionally, NET goes beyond the multiple dimensions of risk that might be modeled in the arbitrage pricing theory (APT). In NET, in addition to systematic risk aversion, investors have a rational aversion to assets that are difficult to diversify, are less liquid, are highly taxed, or are not easily divisible. All of these preferences impact the prices and expected returns of assets that embody these characteristics.

The PAPM goes even further, providing a theory in an equilibrium framework by including both risk aversion and popularity preferences on the part of the investors. These preferences can be rational, as in NET, or irrational, as in behavioral economics. In the PAPM, securities have a variety of characteristics or dimensions of popularity: different systematic or unsystematic risks and a variety of additional attributes that some or all investors care about. All of these characteristics are priced according to the aggregate demand for each of the characteristics. The expected return of each security is determined by its risk and other popularity characteristics.

The concept of a *negative return to popularity* (which we shorten to just "popularity") has been shown to be consistent with the empirical premiums found in the stock market. But it is an explanation after the fact. More direct tests involve identifying in advance what characteristics are likely to be popular and then comparing the performance of stocks that should be unpopular with that of stocks that should be popular based on those characteristics.

We did this for five characteristics. First, we argue that companies with high brand values are popular. These companies end up having significantly lower returns than those with the lowest brand value over our period of study. Second, we argue that companies with wide economic moats, having a sustainable competitive advantage, are more popular. We found that companies with no moat outperform the wide moat companies. Third, we found that companies with a better reputation tend to underperform companies with a worse one. Fourth, we argue that stocks that have had historical negative tail risk events (low or negative coskewness) are unpopular. We found that these stocks significantly outperformed those with high coskewness over the period of study. Finally, we argue that stocks with positive historical skewness are popular because they provide the apparent opportunity for outsized gains. We found that these stocks have the lowest risk-adjusted returns over our period of study.

When we did our five direct tests of the popularity hypothesis, we looked at both equally weighted composites and market capitalization-weighted composites of the stocks, giving us 10 tests. While all results, to a moderate or high degree, were consistent with the popularity hypothesis, only 5 out of 10 were consistent with the "more risk equals more return" paradigm.

We also tested most of the well-known premiums and anomalies for consistency with popularity. We found that low-beta, low-volatility, small-cap, value, and less liquid stocks, being less popular, outperformed their more popular counterparts. To do this, we looked at 10 of the factor tests in Ibbotson and Kim (working paper 2017) through the popularity lens. Of the 10 different factors that we looked at, we found that 7 were consistent with the popularity hypothesis while only 2 were consistent with the "more risk equals more return" paradigm. We also found that within the stock market, the portfolios formed based on these characteristics had an inverse relationship between risk and return, counter to classical theory. Either risk is popular under some circumstances, or other nonrisk characteristics dominate returns. We believe that popularity reflects the demand that ultimately determines prices and returns.

The numerous empirical flaws of the CAPM, and the notion that more risk should equate to more return, have given rise to a variety of behavioral based explanations for observed asset prices. Popularity in general, and the PAPM in particular, unifies the driving factors that impact price in the classical finance CAPM world with those that drive price in a behavioral asset pricing world. In this way, popularity creates a unifying theory—a bridge between classical and behavioral finance.

The publication can be found at

https://www.cfainstitute.org/en/research/foundation/2018/popularity-bridge-between-classical-and-behavioral-finance

Use your mobile device to scan the QR code to go straight to the webpage.

III. LITERATURE REVIEW SUMMARIES

THE CURRENT STATE OF QUANTITATIVE EQUITY INVESTING

by Ying L. Becker and Marc R. Reinganum

Quantitative equity management is concerned with rigorous, disciplined approaches to help investors structure optimal portfolios to achieve the outcomes they seek. At the root of disciplined, modern investment processes are two things: risk and return. The notion of total return is obvious—price appreciation plus any dividend payments. Risk may not be so straightforward. In most quantitative approaches, risk is viewed as more akin to a roulette wheel; that is, the possible outcomes are well specified and the likelihood of each outcome is known, but in advance, an investor does not know which outcome will be realized.

In this piece, we curate the history of quantitative equity investing, which traces its origins to the development of portfolio theory and the capital asset pricing model (CAPM). In equities, some of the first quantitative approaches were aimed at confirming the theoretical predictions of the CAPM. In particular, the expected return of a risky asset depends only on the risk of that asset as measured by its beta, a covariance measure of risk. In this paradigm, all investors hold the same risky portfolio, the market portfolio of risky assets that maximizes the Sharpe ratio. At the same time, stock prices are viewed to be informationally efficient and reflecting all available information.

By the early 1980s, this simple view of the world was punctured by the discovery of stock market anomalies. Researchers discovered that variables other than beta could explain the cross section of expected returns. In particular, size and value were found to contain useful explanatory power. By the 1990s, the anomalies morphed into the mainstream as the anomalies were re-labeled as factors, and the benchmark model, at least in academic research, was a three-factor model with beta, size, and value. Concurrent with the three-factor model, other credible factors muscled their way into the credible empirical asset pricing world, including momentum, liquidity, quality, and volatility. Indeed, in 2011, the president of the American Finance Association described the proliferation of factors as a "zoo of new factors."[1] Recent work suggests using a much higher standard to accept new factors.

With diminishing acceptance of the view that capitalization-weighted indexes are optimal for all investors, factor investing has taken off in practice. Sometime these "smart factors" are called smart beta. Morningstar reported that factor investing is the fastest-growing segment of the investment management marketplace. Investors have recognized that low-cost exposure to other factors might give them superior risk/return trade-offs.

Of course, active investors are still looking for ways to improve performance over more-passive smart beta indexes. In this race, big data approaches offer the potential to grab an insight before it becomes widely known. Another promising avenue is the ability to dynamically adjust allocations to different factors based on the macroeconomic environment and investment conditions. Active managers are also exploring better ways to construct portfolios.

In short, quantitative equity management is alive and well and intellectually active as investors seek to better manage risk and return. Commercially, factor investing has taken off in the form of smart beta. Products and strategies, vetted by decades of prior and current research, are continually being developed. One might reasonably forecast that dynamic factor-timing strategies will be a growth area for the quantitative equity field. A new generation of big data approaches is developing in the field and is likely to grow as technology becomes more capable and more data are digitally available. Despite the advances in theory, modeling, and technology, the goal of quantitative equity management techniques is an old one: aiding investors to achieve more efficient and appropriate investment outcomes.

[1]J. Cochrane, "Presidential Address: Discount Rates," *Journal of Finance* 66 (August 2011): 1047–108.

The publication can be found at
https://www.cfainstitute.org/en/research/foundation/2018/current-state-of-quantitative-equity-investing

Use your mobile device to scan the QR code to go straight to the webpage.

IV. BRIEFS SUMMARIES

FOUNDATIONS OF HIGH-YIELD ANALYSIS

edited by Martin S. Fridson, CFA

Since the advent some 40 years ago of a vibrant primary market for speculative-grade corporate bonds, the high-yield market has evolved from a niche occupied by a small group of specialists into a full-fledged institutional investment category. Asset allocators and portfolio managers now have at their disposal the tools necessary for rigorous investment analysis, including financial statements of the issuers, indexes, trading prices, historical default rates, and time series on such credit factors as liquidity, ratings, and covenant quality. This research brief provides up-to-date techniques for extracting from the extensive data the information that can lead to sound investment decisions.

Conference moderator Martin Fridson, CFA, chief investment officer of Lehmann Livian Fridson Advisors LLC, decomposes long-term returns on high-yield bonds as follows:

(Treasury yield + Spread vs. Treasuries) –
(Default rate + Recovery rate) = Return.

Over shorter periods, Fridson points out, total return can diverge widely from the output of this formula because of changes in the spread-versus-Treasuries and the underlying Treasury yield. As an alternative to gauging the high-yield asset class's value at a point in time by comparing the spread-versus-Treasuries with its historical average, he offers an econometric model that compares the spread with a comprehensive measure of prevailing risk. Fridson cites research documenting the default rate impact of changes in the composition of the high-yield universe. He also emphasizes the variability of recovery rates over the course of the credit cycle. A striking feature of high-yield returns, Fridson observes, is their extraordinary dispersion in contrast to the investment-grade market.

Bill Hoffman, senior analyst at Investcorp Credit Management US LLC, explains the process by which a high-yield analyst decides whether to recommend investment in a new issue. The analysis compares the new issue with issues of similar credits, taking into account macroeconomic factors, industry fundamentals, business-specific risks, and the issuer's financial strategy. Financial strategy comprises free cash flow, deleveraging potential, and the risk of additional leveraging transactions. Hoffman emphasizes that this process is an art, not a science. To illustrate, he provides a case study involving Kraton Performance Polymers' 2015 announcement of the acquisition of Arizona Chemical. His analysis addresses the additional factors of the attractiveness of the business combination and synergies arising from it. Hoffman finds that marketwide technical factors created an exceptional opportunity in the Kraton bond.

Diane Vazza, head of Global Fixed Income Research at Standard & Poor's Global Ratings, outlines her firm's forecasting model for the high-yield default rate. The main components are economic variables, financial variables, bank lending practices, the interest burden of high-yield companies, the slope of the Treasury yield curve, and credit-related variables. Vazza elaborates on how the default rate can be suppressed by easy access to credit for refinancing debt and extending maturities or, alternatively, be elevated by a rise in interest rates following heavy borrowing for leveraged buyouts, share repurchases, and increased dividends rather than investment in conventional business activities. She further describes how the default rate can be affected by dynamics within particular industries that do not spill over into the rest of the high-yield universe. Because default probability is highest among the lowest-rated issuers, the universe's ratings mix also influences the default rate.

Anders Maxwell, Managing Director at PJ Solomon, presents a primer on the legal underpinnings and process of corporate bankruptcy. Emphasizing the centrality of valuing the estate, he explains that to address ambiguities in that task, the court may scrutinize accounting standards, financial projections, and key assumptions underlying competing valuations. Maxwell also describes the conditions under which an out-of-court restructuring is most feasible. He highlights factors that create opportunity in distressed securities, including volatile and uncertain values as a consequence of the opaque and complex dynamics of corporate restructuring, as well as an inefficient market for the securities. Additionally, Maxwell presents two case studies to illustrate the pitfalls of relying on market prices as indications of intrinsic value. One bankrupt company's securities declined prior to the filing and rose afterwards; the other company's securities displayed the opposite pattern.

Saish Setty, director of reorg covenants at Reorg Research, provides a theoretical framework for understanding the need for covenants and lays out the main risks to creditors. He describes some common covenants, including those dealing with debt levels, liens, restricted payments and investments, and asset sales. He shows how covenants are necessitated by shareholder–creditor conflicts and inter-creditor conflicts. The risks arising from such conflicts include incurrence of risky investments by the borrower, subordination and dilution, and value leakage. Setty also explains the two general types of covenants, affirmative and negative, and the significance of restricted and unrestricted subsidiaries. In addition, he highlights potential pitfalls. For example, he states that the so-called hookie dook provision historically common in oil and gas issues arguably gutted the liens covenant. Setty argues that close attention to defined terms, differences among an issuer's outstanding instruments, and interactions among different covenants can help to identify hidden risks in an indenture.

Michael Brown, global head of research at Advantage Data, analyzes high-yield price histories as a function of macroeconomic forces, microeconomic forces, impulse forces (influences that abruptly rise to a peak, then fade gradually), risk, and technical features of the time series themselves. He notes that in the short term, high-yield prices are subject to fluctuations and a high level of noise (random fluctuation). Over longer time intervals, price moves occur at lower frequencies, subject to lower noise and less fluctuation. Brown finds that high-yield prices move in recurring patterns involving trends and cycles. He tells how to filter out the noise and outliers that obscure these patterns. Also, he identifies the most important macro factors in driving fair value. Brown stresses the importance of using as a starting point a price source based on actual trades, such as TRACE (Trade Reporting and Compliance Engine) data for North American bond trades. This information can be supplemented by additional trade-related data—for example, volumes traded and amounts outstanding.

Armed with the analytical methods described in this brief, institutional investors can have confidence in their ability to manage risk in an asset class perhaps better known for its hazards than for its diversifying benefits within a broad portfolio. The contributors also show practitioners how they can potentially exploit inefficiencies in the pricing of individual issues and sectors, as well as the asset class itself. Notwithstanding certain unique features, the high-yield market is analyzable within the same risk–reward framework used for equities, investment-grade bonds, and other institutional categories.

The publication can be found at

https://www.cfainstitute.org/en/research/foundation/2018/foundations-of-high-yield-analysis

Use your mobile device to scan the QR code to go straight to the webpage.

LATIN AMERICAN LOCAL CAPITAL MARKETS: CHALLENGES AND SOLUTIONS

edited by Mauro Miranda, CFA

Economic growth depends on the efficient allocation of resources, including the two main factors of production: labor and capital. Markets, operating on each factor, have allocated these resources in economies worldwide in ways that arguably approach optimality and have fostered economic development for the benefit of billions. Capital markets, both for debt and equity securities, have allowed firms to secure funding for productive uses while providing investors with opportunities for portfolio diversification. The importance of capital markets for the development of economies and for the betterment of society cannot be overstated.

This is just as true in emerging economies with free markets, such as those found in Latin America, as it is in developed markets. However, capital markets in the region are not being utilized to the fullest. What challenges face Latin American countries in the development of their local capital markets? How can these countries unlock the true potential of their markets and thus spur growth?

The idea behind this collection of articles is to offer a primer on the development of local capital markets in several select countries in Latin America. We discuss not only their history and current status but also their future. To this end, seven authors contributed to this project, each writing about one of seven countries: Argentina, Brazil, Chile, Colombia, Mexico, Peru, and Uruguay. Each author decided which issues they believe matter most to the progress of their local capital markets. Some authors chose a qualitative and institutional description of local markets, whereas others adopted a more quantitative approach.

Lionel Modi, CFA, provides an account of the recent evolution of capital markets in Argentina and identifies five stages in their development, culminating with the current stage that has prevailed since 2015. As Mr. Modi shows, in 2016, Argentina emerged from the international debt default status into which it fell in the early 2000s. This recovery was fundamental for attracting foreign investors to Argentina's local markets. His article discusses the main asset classes that exist in Argentina and points out that political commitment and market, tax, and pension system reforms in Argentina will be key to the future growth of its capital markets.

I discuss Brazil's equity and debt capital markets in an article that starts with a brief outline of the way these markets evolved over the past several decades. Although important advancements have occurred in the development of the country's capital markets, macroeconomic issues—including high interest rates, fiscal indiscipline, and the crowding out of private capital markets by public issuance—have constantly challenged such progress. Progress in Brazil also depends on more efficient regulations and financial education. I argue that some of the necessary conditions for the accelerated growth and development of Brazil's capital markets are already in place, so stakeholders must take advantage of current opportunities.

Nicolás Álvarez, CFA, covers the local fixed-income market in Chile. After providing information about the characteristics of, and main players in, that market, Mr. Álvarez offers a quantitative analysis of how the market is integrated with international markets in terms of price co-movement. He also discusses recent changes in the Chilean regulatory environment and indicates that both administrative and tax reporting requirements are now friendlier to investors, especially foreign ones. Challenges that need to be tackled in Chile include the dominance of pension funds and the effect of such dominance on market liquidity and international integration.

César Cuervo, CFA, begins his article on Colombia by stating that there is ample room for growth and improvement in that country's local capital markets. He discusses several issues that are essential to making Colombian capital markets more functional and efficient. Although the local equity market is underdeveloped in terms of the ratio of market capitalization to GDP, the local fixed-income market is relatively robust and liquid, albeit more on the government side than on the corporate side. Mr. Cuervo lists stronger regulator supervision, more formalization in the economy, and better governance regarding voting and nonvoting shares—as well as other changes—as prerequisites for stronger and deeper capital markets in Colombia.

Jorge Unda, CFA, discusses Mexico's recent financial history and its impact on the development of the country's local capital markets. He acknowledges that important structural changes have taken place in the last two decades, including pension reform, the creation of a benchmark yield curve, consolidation in the banking sector, and a commitment to macroeconomic prudence. Although the crowding-out effect exists in Mexico, Mr. Unda argues that the participation of foreign investors has mitigated it. However, predicting the long-term impact of some recent reforms, including those of 2014, is difficult. For Mexico, the key to capital market development—and economic growth—seems to lie with the expansion of credit.

The recent development of the local capital markets in Peru is the theme of Melvin Escudero's article. He argues that a combination of excessive regulation, tax structure, and the predominance of banks in financing activities provides a disincentive for companies to tap the capital markets, affecting the supply side of securities. In addition, the absence of a financial culture, a preference for foreign assets, and taxes on income and capital gains on capital market securities (while bank instruments are tax exempt) have negatively affected the demand side. Given these circumstances, it is not surprising that liquidity in the Peruvian capital markets is thin. Governmental and private sector initiatives are needed to improve this scenario.

Barbara Mainzer, CFA, examines the features that make Uruguay a stable and reliable international center for business. Ms. Mainzer points out that, although the country has a long history in the financial markets, its capital markets are less developed than those of other countries in the region because of the small size of companies, corporate governance issues, and regulatory weaknesses. The primary market is more important than secondary markets, and the issuance and amount of government debt dwarf those of private debt. Still, the high-income investor base, government incentives, and increased participation of private pension funds are attractive elements that can promote the development of local capital markets in Uruguay.

Although capital markets in the countries discussed in this brief differ in their distinctive characteristics, stages of development, and relevance to the local economy, the articles collected here show that these nations share some familiar challenges, including the considerable size of the government bond markets, inadequate or insufficient regulatory oversight, and cultural characteristics that lead investors to look for investment opportunities elsewhere. The articles also share some potential solutions for promoting the accelerated development of local markets, such as economic reforms, increased regulatory efficiency, improved governance, and greater internationalization.

I hope that this publication will add to the debate on how to improve local capital markets and will encourage all stakeholders—especially issuers, investors, and regulators—to collaborate in proposing and implementing those solutions for the benefit of society.

The publication can be found at
https://www.cfainstitute.org/en/research/foundation/2018/latin-american-local-capital-markets

Use your mobile device to scan the QR code to go straight to the webpage.

MAINSTREAMING SUSTAINABLE INVESTING

edited by Michael J. Greis, CFA

"Mainstreaming Sustainable Investing" is the title, tagline, and guiding principle of the annual Sustainable Investing Seminars run by CFA Society Boston since 2013. In that first year, the idea of "mainstreaming" sustainable investing seemed wildly aspirational to many. Yet by the time the society held its fourth annual seminar in November 2016, aspiration had been surpassed by reality, as the increasing attendance and diversity of the audience reflected the change that was underway in the industry.

To put this development into perspective, though, it is necessary to more clearly articulate what is meant by both "mainstreaming" and "sustainable investing."

A simple and widely used definition of sustainability is taken from a 1987 report on sustainable development prepared for the United Nations by the Brundtland Commission: "Sustainable development is development that meets the needs of the present without compromising the ability of future generations to meet their own needs." This definition will sound familiar to investment professionals involved with endowments and families as the concept of *intergenerational equity*.

The purpose of investing is to apply capital to productive use, addressing opportunities and challenges facing societies and economies, thereby building value over time for the investors supplying that capital. But that value-building economic activity does not take place within a hermetically sealed financial system. Value creation takes place in and depends on environmental, social, and governance systems. It requires the assets and resources those systems provide. Economic activity that is not sustainable degrades those systems, diminishing their future viability and value. Sustainable economic activity maintains or enhances those systems, increasing their future viability and value. The future value of the investment depends heavily on the future state of those systems.

The investment profession has a well-developed language and formal system for measuring and assessing the value created (or destroyed) by financial capital. We use these financial factors and indicators in this work. But we do not yet have a similarly robust system for assessing the value created or destroyed by the use or misuse of environmental, social, and governance (ESG) capital. What we do have is an evolving language of ESG issues, factors, and indicators. The core of sustainable investing is incorporating these ESG issues, factors, and indicators into the investment process.

Viewed through this lens, considering the ESG impacts on future value contributes to fulfilling our mandate as investment professionals. As Erika Karp, the opening speaker at the first Sustainable Investing Seminar in 2013, observed, "Sustainable investing is just investing."

In the same way, sustainable investors are not that different from other investors. Sustainable investors seek to

- reduce risk,
- obtain alpha (outperformance),
- engage to improve performance of their investments,
- achieve an economic or societal outcome, and
- invest in ways consistent with their values and beliefs.

Reading this list from the bottom up generates the stereotype of the "sustainable" investor. Similarly, reading from the top down generates the stereotype of the "regular" investor. In both cases, the extreme versions of the stereotype would leave out the later items, resulting in the perception that "sustainable" investors are willing to ignore risk and return, whereas "regular" investors don't care about values or societal outcomes. Both are wrong. Each of these motivations can apply to any investor.

Like all investors, sustainable investors prioritize these motivations and weigh their importance differently. The challenge for sustainable investment professionals is to understand their clients' motivations and then shape their expectations and investment strategy accordingly. Given this range of motivations and the diversity of ESG systems, it should not be surprising that there are many ways to approach investing sustainably.

Mainstreaming sustainable investing is, therefore, not found as a definitive recipe of three parts "E," one part "S," and two parts "G." Nor is it found in a broad claim of being a "sustainable" or "responsible" investor. Mainstreaming is achieved when ESG issues, factors, tools, and techniques are applied throughout investment practice in support of client requirements.

The 2016 seminar showcased how deeply and broadly ESG issues have reached into the profession of investment management. This research brief, comprising articles written by speakers at the 2016 Sustainable Investing Seminar, showcases the significantly increased activity and innovation taking place and the wide-ranging impact sustainable investing is having on the investment profession.

At the 2015 Sustainable Investing Seminar, Jean Rogers, founder and former CEO of the Sustainable Accounting Standards Board, highlighted new research from George Serafeim, a professor at Harvard Business School. Professor Serafeim's research showed that firms with good ratings on material sustainability issues significantly outperform firms with poor ratings on such issues. A subsequent paper by Serafeim, published shortly before he spoke at the 2016 seminar, extended that research to shareholder engagement and provided evidence that filing shareholder proposals on material ESG issues was associated with an increase in Tobin's *q*. This research is part of the growing body of work collected over the last five years that demonstrates that ESG information is value relevant.

In his article for this brief, Professor Serafeim moves beyond this important but static analysis at the company level to the broader value of ESG information in assessing the impact of transformational changes in the economy. Using mobility as a case study of large-scale transformation driven by technology and climate change, he describes how robust ESG information on material issues will be necessary to understand which organizations will be successful and how to deploy capital in markets.

The amount and complexity of financial data available to analysts soared during the later years of the 20th century. A parallel explosion in information technology enabled the growth in quantitative approaches to investing. The rapid growth in the availability of ESG information in recent years has led to the emergence of quantitative ESG strategies. However, it can be challenging to process such an overwhelming amount of data from both financial and non-financial sources. The relatively higher proportion of qualitative and unstructured data makes the challenge even greater.

Leveraging the power of big data and machine learning to address this opportunity is the subject of Andreas Feiner's article. Feiner, a founding partner and head of ESG research and advisory at Arabesque Asset Management, describes the development of S-Ray, a tool that aggregates large volumes of sustainability information and applies customizable rules-based analysis on a continuous basis to provide daily snapshots of a company's sustainability. He provides an example of applying values-neutral, unbiased algorithms to generate performance in a values-based context.

For investment practitioners learning about ESG, the first and dominant narrative is about the impact of ESG factors on companies and stock prices, especially large-cap public equities, although rapid growth in green bonds has brought increased attention to fixed income and ESG. It is not surprising, then, that analyzing the impact of ESG factors is much more common in valuing equities than in valuing fixed-income securities. Going a step beyond that—considering factor impacts for a portfolio of equities and fixed-income securities—is complex even in mainstream financial analysis.

Professor Andreas Hoepner of University College Dublin addresses this issue through the emerging discipline of "financial data science." Financial data science applies advanced statistical analysis to very large amounts of real-world data. It seeks to use the explanatory power of the data in predicting outcomes to suggest appropriate actions and guide further research. In his article, Professor Hoepner considers the integration of ESG issues into a mixed assets universe, where equity and fixed-income securities are examined in one analytical setting. Which of the dozens of ESG issues perform well in both equity and fixed-income securities, and especially in the mixed setting? The results are surprising, especially with regard to governance issues.

Steve Lydenberg, CFA, a partner at Domini Social Investments, wrapped up the first Sustainable Investing Seminar in 2013 with a discussion of the challenges and opportunities for security analysts as ESG disclosure inevitably becomes universal, based on standardized metrics, and integrated into financial reporting. For more than 30 years, Lydenberg has been a pioneer in sustainable investing, consistently and presciently identifying and tackling the next challenge in the evolution of the field.

In his article, Lydenberg observes how our understanding of risk and the tools to manage it have evolved—from considering the risk of a single security to risk at the portfolio level. He argues that we must now consider system-wide risk.

By complementing the efficient discipline of portfolio management with certain specific intentional actions, investors can manage risks and rewards at these system-related levels, as well as within their portfolios. System-level considerations have the potential to generate a "smart beta" play, with the management of risks and rewards at these levels increasing the performance of whole indexes, as opposed to helping generate increased "alpha" for individual portfolios.

The topics considered in these articles—transformational economic change, quantitative investing, performance of a multi-asset-class portfolio, and systemic risk management as a source of smart beta—demonstrate the ongoing mainstreaming of sustainable investing.

At the same time, each topic builds upon a robust base of ESG concepts that definitively place them within a values-based framework of sustainable investing. Or, to quote Karp once again, "sustainable investing is just investing."

The publication can be found at
https://www.cfainstitute.org/en/research/foundation/2018/mainstreaming-sustainable-investing

Use your mobile device to scan the QR code to go straight to the webpage.

RISK TOLERANCE AND CIRCUMSTANCES

by Elke U. Weber and Joachim Klement, CFA

The term *risk tolerance* is defined and used in different ways. Whether risk tolerance is a stable characteristic of a given investor or also takes into account external circumstances (e.g., economic shocks or the domain of the decision) depends on how it is defined and measured. This brief focuses on a definition of risk tolerance prevalent in the practitioner community—namely, an investor's willingness to take perceived risk or the trade-off an investor is willing to make between the perceived risk and expected return of different investment choices. This definition derives from a psychological interpretation of the risk–return framework of classical portfolio theory. It treats risk tolerance as an *attitude toward risk* and decouples this pure attitudinal variable from the *perceptions of risks and returns*—psychological variables in their own right and distinct from the expected value and variance of the distribution of possible outcomes.

Defined in this way, risk tolerance may differ among investors as a function of socioeconomic and biological differences but (with the exception of a brief boost during adolescence) shows stability across an investor's lifespan, financial shocks, and other circumstances. Risk tolerance, in this sense, is the mediator that translates perceptions of risk and situational needs and constraints into decision and action.

The variables that change with market conditions and other circumstances are investors' perceptions of investment risks and expectations of return. In contrast to risk tolerance, which attaches to an individual and her biological makeup and personality, these variables change over time in response to changing external conditions. Therefore, an investor's risk-taking behavior (as revealed by her investment decisions) can look like it has changed, despite the stability in her risk tolerance. Perceived risks and expected returns are influenced by hopes and fears as much as by past returns and rational expectations and thus need to be assessed in their own right and possibly corrected.

Managing investor emotions through the ups and downs of financial markets is arguably a financial adviser's most important task. Calm times provide an opportunity to discuss and formulate an investment policy for each client that can be consulted when emotions are running high. Managing risk perceptions requires the financial adviser to act more like a therapist than a mechanic. It is above all about managing expectations and emotions and helping clients to better deal with emotions when it comes to financial decisions. The end result of this process might be a portfolio that is not "optimal" in the sense of modern portfolio theory, with its assumption of econs, but rather a portfolio that "satisfies" the human need for investments that can be handled in the presence of changing emotions and changing risk perceptions.

The publication can be found at

https://www.cfainstitute.org/en/research/foundation/2018/risk-tolerance-and-circumstances

Use your mobile device to scan the QR code to go straight to the webpage.

RISK PROFILING AND TOLERANCE: INSIGHTS FOR THE PRIVATE WEALTH MANAGER

edited by Joachim Klement, CFA

If risk aversion and willingness to take on risk are driven by emotions and we as humans are bad at correctly identifying the emotions, then the finance profession has a serious challenge at hand: how to identify reliably the individual risk profile of a retail investor or high-net-worth individual. In this series of CFA Institute Research Foundation briefs, we have asked academics and practitioners to summarize the current state of knowledge about risk profiling in different key areas.

This series, which began in 2015 and continued through 2018, launched with "Investor Risk Profiling: An Overview." In this brief, author Joachim Klement, CFA, determines that the current standard process of risk profiling through questionnaires is highly unreliable and typically explains less than 15% of the variation in risky assets between investors—mostly because the questionnaires focus on socioeconomic variables and hypothetical scenarios. However, the existing research in risk profiling shows that several factors can provide more accurate and reliable insights into the risk profile of investors. Among these factors are the investor's lifetime experiences and past financial decisions as well as the influence of family, friends, and advisers. By using these factors, practitioners can better understand their clients' preferences and recommend suitable investment strategies and products.

In "Risk Profiling through a Behavioral Finance Lens," published in 2016, author Michael Pompian, CFA, examines risk profiling through a behavioral finance lens. Behavioral finance attempts to understand and explain actual investor behavior, in contrast to theorizing about investor behavior. It differs from traditional (or standard) finance, which is based on assumptions of how investors and markets should behave. Much has been written about the tension that exists between the willingness to take risks and the ability to take risks—risk *appetite* is the former and risk *capacity* is the latter. In the behavioral context, risk appetite and risk capacity are defined in terms of known risks and unknown risks. Irrational client behavior often occurs when a client experiences unknown risks. To aid in the advisory process, advisors can use behavioral-investor types to help make rapid yet insightful assessments of what type of investor they are dealing with before recommending an investment plan. With a better understanding of behavioral finance vis-à-vis risk taking, practitioners can enhance their understanding of client preferences and better inform their recommendations of investment strategies and products.

From 2017, in "Financial Risk Tolerance: A Psychometric Review," author John E. Grable provides financial analysts, investment professionals, and financial planners with a review of how financial risk-tolerance tests can and should be evaluated. He begins by clarifying terms related to risk taking and then provides a broad overview of two important measurement terms: validity and reliability. He concludes with examples for practice.

In "Risk Tolerance and Circumstances," published in 2018, authors Elke U. Weber and Joachim Klement, CFA, determine that an investor's risk attitude is a stable characteristic, like a personality trait, but that risk-taking behavior can change based on the investor's age, recent market events, and life experiences. These factors change investors' perceptions of risks. Differences in risk tolerance between men and women or in different circumstances trace back to emotional as much as rational considerations. Financial advisers should consider all of these factors when advising clients and can use four simple steps to incorporate best practices: be aware, educate, nudge, and hand hold.

Finally, in the 2017 publication "New Vistas in Risk Profiling," author Greg B. Davies explains that risk profiling is fraught with misunderstandings that lead to ill-advised approaches to determining suitable investment solutions for individuals. The author discusses how we should think about the crucial elements of (a) risk tolerance, (b) behavioral risk attitudes, and (c) risk capacity. He uses a simple thought experiment to examine a stripped-down investor situation and define the essential features and exact role of each of the components of an investor's overall risk profile. Davies concludes by examining options for eliciting and measuring risk tolerance and considering some promising avenues for future methods.

The publication can be found at
https://www.cfainstitute.org/en/research/foundation/2018/risk-profiling-and-tolerance

Use your mobile device to scan the QR code to go straight to the webpage.

SOME LIKE IT HEDGED

by Momtchil Pojarliev

Foreign currency exposure is a by-product of international investing. When obtaining global asset exposure, investors also obtain the embedded foreign currency exposure. Left unmanaged, this currency exposure acts like a buy-and-hold currency strategy, which receives little or no risk premium and adds unwanted volatility. In "Some Like It Hedged," the author shows that the impact of foreign currency exposure on institutional portfolios depends significantly on the base currency of the investors and the specific composition of their portfolios. In general, investors whose base currency is negatively correlated with global equities, as are the US dollar and the Japanese yen, will reduce the volatility of their portfolios by fully hedging foreign currency exposure. In contrast, investors whose home currency is positively correlated with global equities, as is the Canadian dollar, will benefit from keeping some unhedged foreign currency exposure—in particular, exposure to the US dollar. Finally, investors with larger allocations to domestic assets will experience only small reductions in volatility from hedging.

Pojarliev discusses a variety of options to address foreign currency exposures. Although there is no single best-practice solution for addressing foreign currency exposures, institutional investors have three main choices.

1. Do nothing (i.e., maintain unhedged foreign currency exposure). Doing nothing is always the easiest option, but from a risk–return perspective, it could be the worst available choice. Currency has no long-term expected return because, although it is a risk exposure, it is not an economic

asset. Hence, long-term currency returns are expected to be zero. Hedging should, therefore, have no long-term impact on the return and only affect the volatility. The volatility reduction from hedging can be redeployed more efficiently by increasing exposure to economic assets for which a risk premium exists.

2. Hedge passively (i.e., maintain a constant hedge ratio).In general, hedging some of the foreign currency risk will decrease the volatility of the portfolio. The relationship between a specific hedge ratio and the decrease in volatility depends on the particular portfolio and, most importantly, on the base currency of the investor. Yet, passive hedging creates its own problems, including negative cash flow generation when foreign currencies are appreciating and detraction from returns because of hedging costs. Passive hedging might also introduce a major market-timing risk. If the base currency weakens after a passive policy is implemented, the investor will suffer substantial hedging losses when the forward currency hedging contracts settle.

3. Hedge actively (i.e., vary the hedge ratio). One way to address the market-timing risk of implementing a passive hedging program is to actively time the hedging of the foreign currencies. An active hedging program seeks to reduce the risk of the foreign currency exposure but varies the hedge ratios for the various currencies based on market views to avoid negative cash flow and to generate positive returns. A successful active hedging program should both add to the return of the portfolio and lower the volatility, and it should outperform both an unhedged and a passive hedging benchmark.

The best choice to address foreign currency exposure will differ from institution to institution, but it boils down to two fundamental factors. First, the optimal solution depends on the importance of risk versus return and the institution's tolerance for negative cash flow. Second, investors must decide whether they believe that currency managers are able to achieve a positive information ratio over the long run after fees and, importantly, whether they will be able to identify these currency managers. Any currency policy will depend on the details of the specific portfolio—in particular, on the base currency of the investor and the size of the foreign currency exposure.

The publication can be found at
https://www.cfainstitute.org/en/research/foundation/2018/some-like-it-hedged

Use your mobile device to scan the QR code to go straight to the webpage.

V. MULTIMEDIA SUMMARIES

THE FUTURE OF INVESTMENT MANAGEMENT: IN BRIEF

Ronald N. Kahn

Investment management is in flux, arguably more than it has been in a long time. Active management is under pressure, with investors switching from active to index funds. New "smart beta" products offer low-cost exposures to many active ideas. Exchange-traded funds are proliferating. Markets and regulations have changed significantly over the past 10–20 years, and data and technology—which are increasingly important for investment management—are evolving even more rapidly.

In the midst of this change, what can we say about the future of investment management? What ideas will influence its evolution? What types of products will flourish over the next 5–10 years?

I use a long perspective to address these questions and analyze the modern intellectual history of investment management—the set of ideas that have influenced investment management up to now.

One central theme that emerges is that investment management is becoming increasingly systematic. Our understanding of risk has evolved from a general aversion to losing money to a precisely defined statistic we can measure and forecast. Our understanding of expected returns has evolved as the necessary data have become more available, as our understanding of fundamental value has developed, and as we have come to understand the connection between return and risk and the relevance of human behavior to both. Data and technology have advanced in parallel to facilitate implementing better approaches.

With an understanding of the ideas underlying investment management today, including several insights into active management, I discuss the many trends currently roiling the field. These trends, applied to the current state of investment management, suggest that investment management will evolve into three distinct branches—indexing, smart beta/factor investing, and pure alpha investing. Each branch will offer two styles of products: those that focus exclusively on returns and those that include goals beyond returns.

To view the video, visit:

https://www.cfainstitute.org/en/research/multimedia/2018/the-future-of-investment-management

The publication can be found at

https://www.cfainstitute.org/en/research/foundation/2018/future-of-investment-management.

2008 FINANCIAL CRISIS: A TEN-YEAR REVIEW

The Research Foundation was pleased to co-sponsor the two-day conference 2008 Financial Crisis: A Ten-Year Review. The conference was hosted in conjunction with Annual Reviews, the New York University Stern School of Business, and the MIT Golub Center for Finance and Policy (GCFP).

8 November 2018

"Opening Remarks," Raghu Sundaram, NYU Stern School of Business

Sundaram opens the conference by recalling the events of the Great Financial Crisis (GFC). "That whole period," he says, "every month, every day, was a period of wonder at what is happening in financial markets." With each new development, it seemed the conventional understanding of the financial markets was undermined. But the financial crisis also created unprecedented critical reflection on what had gone wrong and unprecedented engagement among researchers, policy makers, and academics to answer that question, Sundaram observes, with NYU Stern at the forefront of those efforts. This conference, he says, will showcase some of the key economic insights that have developed in the aftermath of the crisis.

To view the video, visit:

https://www.cfainstitute.org/research/multimedia/2018/2008-financial-crisis-review-opening-remarks

"Introduction to the Annual Review of Financial Economics," Andrew Lo, MIT

Lo presents a history of Annual Reviews, particularly the Annual Review of Financial Economics, which he co-edits with Robert Merton, and he discusses his own analysis of scholarship on the financial crisis.

To view the video, visit:

https://www.cfainstitute.org/research/multimedia/2018/2008-financial-crisis-intro-to-annual-review-financial-economics

"Deglobalization: The Rise of Disembedded Unilateralism," Harold James, Princeton

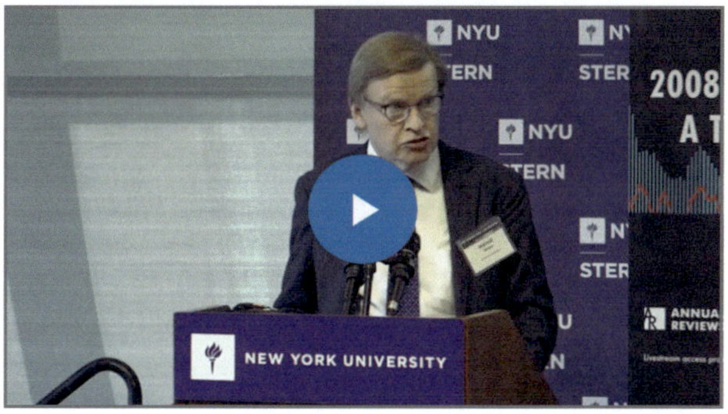

James leads off his presentation with a "Game of Thrones" reference: "Winter is coming." He sees the financial crisis as having initiated the dismantling of the post-World War II Bretton Woods consensus of embedded liberalism, in which peace and prosperity were seen as inseparable and globalism was embraced. What's taking its place is "a vision of extreme realism in political science" that he calls "disembedded unilateralism." This zero-sum approach—typified by trade wars, border walls, and Brexit—has rendered the dominant center-right and center-left political party dynamic of the last 70 years obsolete. Pointing to Brexit, James observes that it is counterproductive to Labour and Tory alike. James holds out hope, however, that efforts to dismantle globalization may paradoxically lead to its reform and renaissance.

To view the video, visit:

https://www.cfainstitute.org/research/multimedia/2018/2008-financial-crisis-deglobalization

"Trust and the Future of Finance," Robert Merton, MIT

The financial crisis led to a loss of trust in providers, regulators, and financial innovation among consumers, Merton observes. Some have proposed technology can stand in for trust, but he says fintech cannot create trust or succeed without it. Two things, however, can substitute for trust: verification and transparency. Some forms of fintech can provide verification, but financial advice tends to be opaque rather than transparent. Merton also discusses data showing retail investors as less satisfied with cost disclosures and performance from active portfolio managers than institutional investors.

To view the video, visit:

https://www.cfainstitute.org/research/multimedia/2018/2008-financial-crisis-trust-and-future-finance

"Architecture and Stability of the Financial System," Franklin Allen, Imperial College

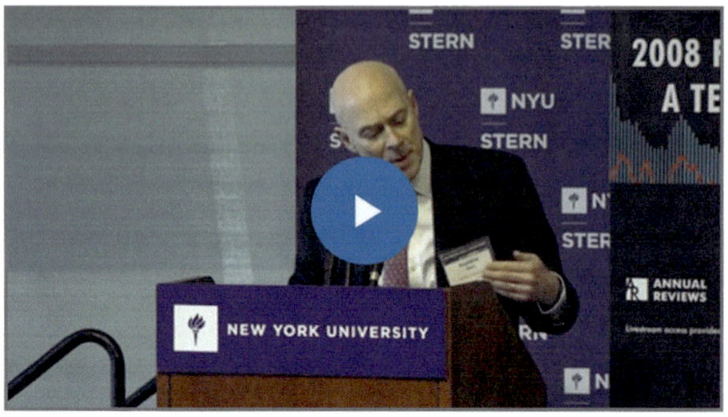

Many different aspects of financial architecture have been associated with assorted financial stability issues, Allen says. These include the exchange rate system with currency and sovereign debt crises; financial market structures with stock market crashes; and banks versus non-bank intermediaries with non-bank runs. He goes on to chart the literature on financial architecture and offers his own insights into testing for stability.

Ansgar Walther, Allen's co-author on the paper, then takes the podium to talk about financial architecture in non-bank intermediaries—asset managers, in particular.

To view the video, visit:

https://www.cfainstitute.org/research/multimedia/2018/2008-financial-crisis-architecture-stability-financial-system

"Financial Crises," Gary Gorton, Yale

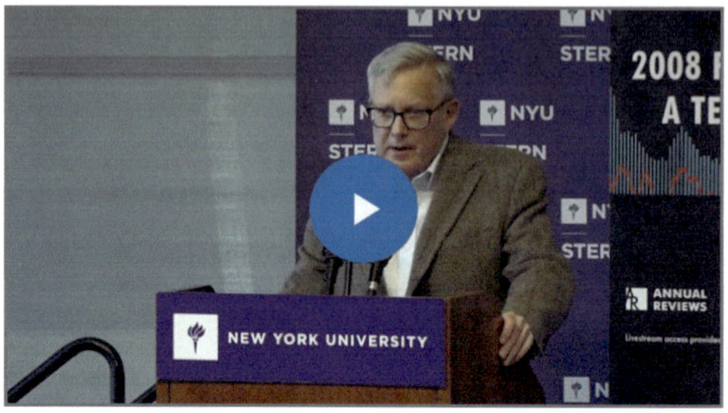

"Financial crises are not rare," Gorton says, noting that 147 systemic events have occurred since 1970. They generally come about when people no longer believe their banks are safe and thus want their money en masse, creating a run on the banks. History suggests that financial crises are inevitable because new forms of short-term debt continually transform the system, Gorton says. But regulation can potentially cushion these blows. Of course, there may be a tradeoff between crisis-avoiding regulations and economic growth.

To view the video, visit:

https://www.cfainstitute.org/research/multimedia/2018/2008-financial-crisis-financial-crises

"Accounting Issues that Impact Financial Stability," Stephen Ryan, NYU

"Bank financial reporting requirements and practices affect financial stability," Ryan says. "But these effects are often misunderstood, overstated, or otherwise mischaracterized." Ryan discusses the three main bank financial reporting areas and their alleged shortcomings.

To view the video, visit:

https://www.cfainstitute.org/research/multimedia/2018/2008-financial-crisis-accounting-issues

"Deregulating Wall Street," Kim Schoenholtz, NYU

Discussing topics from the paper he co-authored with Matthew Richardson and Lawrence White, Schoenholtz considers the strengths and weaknesses of Dodd–Frank financial regulations and the efforts to scale back the legislation. He outlines five key takeaways and considers new emerging risks and what might be done to counteract them.

To view the video, visit:

https://www.cfainstitute.org/research/multimedia/2018/2008-financial-crisis-deregulating-wall-street

"Causes and Consequences of Mortgage Defaults," Christopher Foote, Federal Reserve Bank of Boston

Foote discusses his joint paper with Paul Willen, which explores the connections among the housing cycle, the recession, and mortgage defaults. A chief area of focus is the relationship among underwater mortgages, adverse life events, and defaults.

To view the video, visit:

https://www.cfainstitute.org/research/multimedia/2018/2008-financial-crisis-causes-consequences-mortgage-defaults

"Housing Markets," Antoinette Schoar, MIT

Schoar talks about the role of housing markets in the run up to and in the aftermath of the crisis—the topic of the paper she co-authored with Manuel Adelino and Felipe Severino. Her main point is that the prevailing narratives about the housing crisis are largely incorrect. The crisis was not chiefly driven by subprime mortgages or lower income cohorts. Instead, she concludes that a major culprit was optimistic house price expectations, which led to an expansion of credit and delinquencies.

To view the video, visit:

https://www.cfainstitute.org/research/multimedia/2018/2008-financial-crisis-housing-markets

"Measuring the Cost of Bailouts," Deborah Lucas, MIT

Lucas sets out to define and measure bailouts, a process that is much more subtle than meets the eye. In the aftermath of GFC-related bailouts, competing narratives surfaced: The public paid untold billions in unfair bailouts of financial institutions, or the bailouts were paid back with interest. Bailouts tend to be measured in three different ways, Lucas says: fair value cost as of the time of the bailout; fair value cost ex ante as of the time of a granted subsidized guarantee; or sum up ex post realized cash flows. The example of the largest bailout, of Fannie Mae and Freddie Mac, demonstrates the huge variations depending on the method, Lucas notes: The fair value cost was $311 billion; ex ante was $8 billion; and ex post the government made $58 billion. Lucas herself calculates the direct cost of bailouts at around $500 billion, or 3.5% of 2009 GDP.

To view the video, visit:

https://www.cfainstitute.org/research/multimedia/2018/2008-financial-crisis-measuring-cost-bailouts

Fireside Chat with Peter Hancock, former president and CEO of AIG, and Gillian Tett, Financial Times

Hancock, who took the helm at AIG in February 2010, discusses his role in "putting Humpty Dumpty back together again," in an interview with Tett. His task was especially difficult, he says, because of the degree of vilification. AIG was a poster child, rightly or wrongly, for the excesses that brought on the financial crisis. Hancock set out to restore trust in AIG and stave off liquidation. That meant 120 board meetings in a single year and countless negotiations with government agencies. "We had to persuade people that the whole was worth more than the sum of its parts," he says. AIG insured 100,000s of businesses that would have fallen if the company hadn't been saved. The government bailout was paid back in full in November 2012, according to Hancock. "Part of what we saved is still the largest insurance company in the world," he says.

To view the video, visit:

https://www.cfainstitute.org/research/multimedia/2018/2008-financial-crisis-fireside-chat-peter-hancock

"Reflections on the Financial Crisis," Myron Scholes, Stanford

Scholes presents his research into what the markets were saying about the risks in the S&P 500 in the years before, during, and after the financial crisis, focusing on two-month put options. He concentrates on the tails of the distributions. "When tail events occur," Scholes says, "then risky assets all behave as one." He notes the cliché that 'diversification is free' and instead observes, "In times of stress, it isn't enough." He highlights four distinct periods in the data, which cover the years 2005 to 2009.

To view the video, visit:

https://www.cfainstitute.org/research/multimedia/2018/2008-financial-crisis-reflections-on-financial-crisis

9 November 2018

"Keynote Address: Short-Term Debt, Liquidity, and the Financial Crisis," Douglas Diamond, University of Chicago

Diamond's presentation focuses on bank runs and problems of short-term debt and how they can inform our understanding of the financial crisis—indeed, all financial crises—and whether the measures taken to design more fail-safe financial architecture post-crisis were sufficient. As he states, "Private financial crises are everywhere and always due to problems of short-term debt." He focuses his analysis on runs on money market funds and the role of excess liquidity in shoring up the system.

To view the video, visit:

https://www.cfainstitute.org/research/multimedia/2018/2008-financial-crisis-keynote-short-term-debt-liquidity-financial-crisis

"Intermediary Asset Pricing and the Financial Crisis," Arvind Krishnamurthy, Stanford

Krishnamurthy talks about two things from his paper co-authored with Zhiguo He: academic/research progress inspired by the financial crisis and measurement. In 2005 and 2006, he says, people thought about asset pricing largely through the prism of the Campbell–Cochrane consumption habits model and the long-run risk model of Bansal and Yaron. There's virtue in these models, Krishnamurthy says, but they're "like looking at the world through a telescope from Mars." He goes on to provide a sampling of the new models that have emerged since the crisis and discusses different ways to measure risk.

To view the video, visit:

https://www.cfainstitute.org/research/multimedia/2018/2008-financial-crisis-intermediary-asset-pricing

"Leverage," Tobias Adrian, IMF

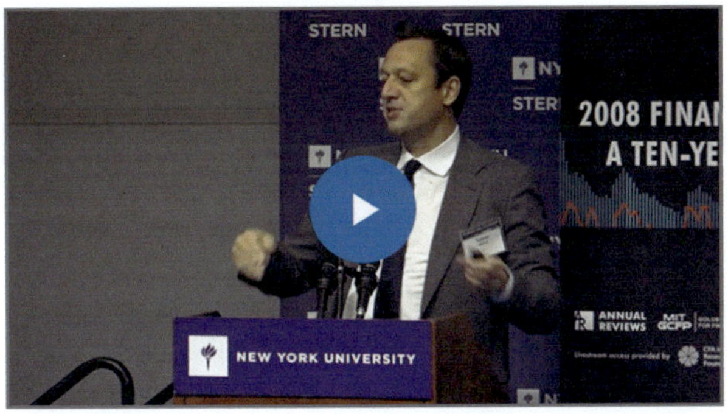

Adrian's presentation focuses on theories of financial crisis. He and his co-authors, Hyun Song Shin and John Kiff, theorize that the financial crisis was a product of the leverage cycle. He notes that leverage has declined since the crisis even amidst an extended economic expansion and an era of easy credit. Adrian believes that new regulations have tamed the leverage cycle and created a safer system, albeit with some unintended consequences that are nevertheless acceptable in terms of magnitude.

To view the video, visit:

https://www.cfainstitute.org/research/multimedia/2018/2008-financial-crisis-leverage

"Systemic Risk," Robert Engle, NYU

"Is the financial system going to erupt again or not?" Engle asks. He addresses that question and discusses the monitoring tools available to measure systemic risk, including those on the Volatility Laboratory (V-Lab) website. Much of his emphasis is on the systemic risk, or SRISK, metric, which seeks to answer the question of how much capital a financial institution would need to raise to function normally in the event of another financial crisis. He concludes, "I think we've some things to worry about. I'll leave you with that."

To view the video, visit:

https://www.cfainstitute.org/research/multimedia/2018/2008-financial-crisis-systemic-risk

"Regulatory Reform," Andrew Metrick, Yale

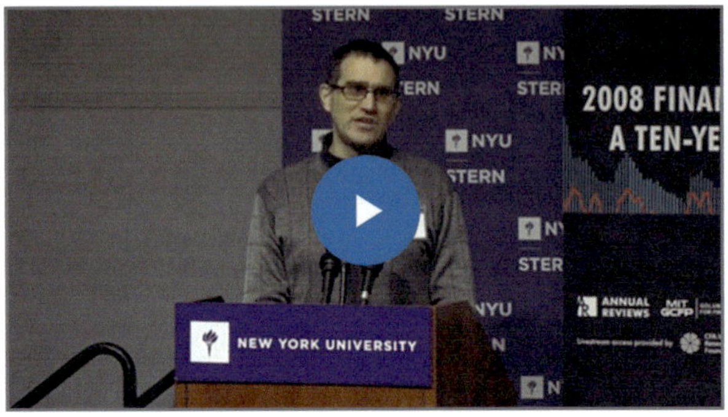

Metrick talks about "some open questions in financial regulations—systemic risk regulations, in particular." His presentation is derived from a paper he co-authored with June Rhee. Metrick doesn't think there's much incentive for researchers to delve into this area, so he describes his presentation as "a much more depressing talk" than the earlier ones. He goes on to define systemic risk, discuss the post-GFC regulatory changes, and present six open questions related to the regulation of systemic risk.

To view the video, visit:

https://www.cfainstitute.org/research/multimedia/2018/2008-financial-crisis-regulatory-reform

"The Role of Central Banking in Crisis Management"

Moderator: Stanley Fischer

Panel: Ben Bernanke, former chair of the US Federal Reserve Board of Governors

Mervyn King, former governor of the Bank of England

Jean-Claude Trichet, former president of the European Central Bank

Fischer, himself former governor of the Bank of Israel and former vice chair of the US Federal Reserve Board of Governors, introduces the three heads of the major central banks during the financial crisis. Their discussion focuses on the causes and nature of the crisis, the lessons they learned, and what they would each do differently.

One of the chief points Bernanke emphasizes is distinguishing between a financial crisis, which he describes as any kind of big shock to the financial system, and a panic, which is a general run on intermediaries and a very particular kind of crisis. In the United States, "The panic was the most important thing," he says. He doesn't think the Great Recession would have been so severe without it. His recommendation: "In the crisis, look for the short-term liabilities, look for where the run potential is." He also stresses how critical it is for central bankers to have robust lender of last resort tools to guard against future panics.

"The essence of this was a run," King says. "The impact on the economy was based on that run." His major takeaways are that the banking system was undercapitalized, lender of last resort facilities were inadequate, and politics were problematic.

One of the major lessons for Trichet was the speed with which the run took place. It created an unprecedented contagion. "The herd formed up in one day," he says. And while he acknowledges that we are safer today, he still sees some of the same issues. "We are still in this interconnection, and we have to prepare." He stresses the importance of maintaining central bank independence. He also points out the resilience of the often-maligned eurozone. Although 5 of the 19 countries had a dramatic crisis, the union still held.

To view the video, visit:

https://www.cfainstitute.org/research/multimedia/2018/2008-financial-crisis-role-central-banking-in-crisis-management

Conference Summary, Stanley Fischer

Fischer sums up the discussion and thanks the panelists, who he says staved off a second Great Depression. While applauding all these efforts, he also notes that they were not enough. "I believe there is a clear link between the populism that is seen now and the fact that we were not able to handle this crisis without major economies going through massive difficulties," he says. "I suspect the very good results of what we did were not enough to keep the Western countries, the leading democracies, on the path they had succeeded in laying out after World War II and continued to pursue until very recently. And I very much doubt that we'd be in this position without the Great Financial Crisis and the Great Recession."

To view the video, visit:

https://www.cfainstitute.org/research/multimedia/2018/2008-financial-crisis-conference-summary

Closing Remarks, Andrew Lo

Lo closes out the conference by thanking all the participants. He also recalls the toll of the crisis and stresses that far from a celebration, this meeting is meant as an opportunity for soul-searching, to better understand the crisis, and to make sure it either does not occur again or that we are prepared when it does.

To view the video, visit:

https://www.cfainstitute.org/research/multimedia/2018/2008-financial-crisis-closing-remarks

VI. WORKSHOP FOR THE PRACTITIONER SUMMARIES

ACTIVE INDEXING: HOW ETF INVESTING HAS IMPACTED INVESTMENT MANAGEMENT

Joanne M. Hill

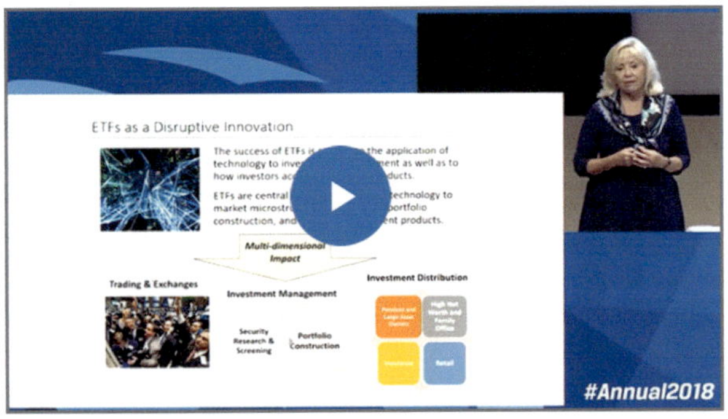

This presentation for the 2018 CFA Institute Research Foundation Workshop for the Practitioner addressed issues covered in our book *A Comprehensive Guide to Exchange-Traded Funds (ETFs)*.[2]

Exchange-traded funds (ETFs) have become in their 25-year history one of the fastest growing segments of the investment management business. These funds provide liquid access to virtually every financial market and allow large and small investors to build institutional-caliber portfolios. Yet, their management fees are significantly lower than those typical of mutual funds. High levels of transparency in ETFs for holdings and investment strategy help investors evaluate an ETF's potential returns and risks. This book covers the evolution of ETFs as products and in their uses in investment strategies. It details how ETFs work, their unique investment and trading features, their regulatory structure, how they are used in tactical and strategic portfolio management in a broad range of asset classes, and how to evaluate them individually.

To view the video, visit:

https://www.cfainstitute.org/en/research/foundation/practitioner-workshops

The publication can be found at:

https://www.cfainstitute.org/en/research/foundation/2015/a-comprehensive-guide-to-exchange-traded-funds-etfs

[2]Co-authors Dave Nadig and Matt Hougan. The book includes an appendix on international ETFs by Deborah Fuhr.

ALTERNATIVE INVESTMENTS: A PRIMER FOR INVESTMENT PROFESSIONALS

Keith Black, CFA, CAIA

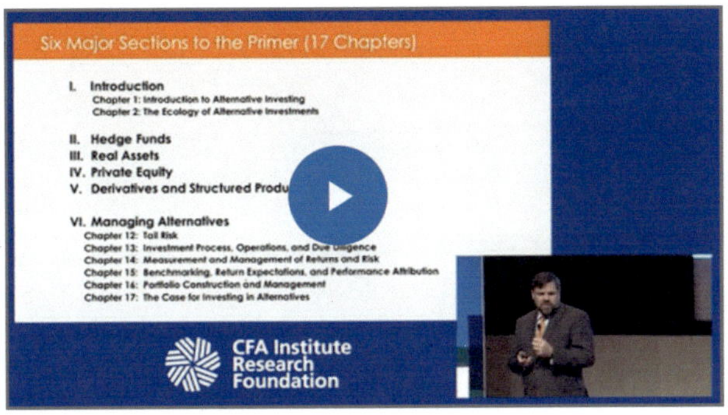

This presentation for the 2018 CFA Institute Research Foundation Workshop for the Practitioner addressed issues covered in our book *Alternative Investments: A Primer for Investment Professionals.*[3]

Alternative Investments: A Primer for Investment Professionals provides an overview of alternative investments for institutional asset allocators and other overseers of portfolios containing both traditional and alternative assets. It is designed for those with substantial experience regarding traditional investments in stocks and bonds but limited familiarity regarding alternative assets, alternative strategies, and alternative portfolio management.

The primer categorizes alternative assets into four groups: hedge funds, real assets, private equity, and structured products/derivatives. Real assets include vacant land, farmland, timber, infrastructure, intellectual property, commodities, and private real estate. For each group, the primer provides essential information about the characteristics, challenges, and purposes of these institutional-quality alternative assets in the context of a well-diversified institutional portfolio.

Other topics addressed by this primer include tail risk, due diligence of the investment process and operations, measurement and management of risks and returns, setting return expectations, and portfolio construction. The primer concludes with a chapter on the case for investing in alternatives.

To view the video, visit:

https://www.cfainstitute.org/en/research/foundation/practitioner-workshops

The publication can be found at:

https://www.cfainstitute.org/en/research/foundation/2018/alternative-investments-a-primer-for-investment-professionals

[3]Co-authors Donald R. Chambers, CAIA, and Nelson J. Lacey, CFA.

VII. AWARDS AND RECOGNITION

JAMES R. VERTIN AWARD

The James R. Vertin Award is presented periodically to recognize individuals who have produced a body of research notable for its relevance and enduring value to investment professionals. This award was established in 1996 to honor James R. Vertin, CFA, for his outstanding leadership in promoting excellence and relevancy in research and education.

2018 Award Winner

William N. Goetzmann

Professor William N. Goetzmann was the recipient of the 2018 James R. Vertin Award for outstanding research. Goetzmann was selected for his noteworthy contributions to the investment profession, including his current research focused on alternative investing, behavioral finance, and the art market. Goetzmann's work also includes studies of stock market predictability, hedge funds, and survival biases in performance measurement. Goetzmann is a distinguished writer, having written and co-authored a number of books, including the recently released *Money Changes Everything: How Finance Made Civilization Possible.*

"Professor Goetzmann is a true Renaissance man whose interests range from the ancient and medieval roots of finance to the design of data graphics," said Larry Siegel, research director, CFA Institute Research Foundation. "The field of finance has been enriched by his detailed study of financial history and talented ability to bring many different fields of knowledge to bear on his research and writing. We thank and congratulate Professor Goetzmann for his significant contributions to the investment management industry."

RESEARCH FOUNDATION SOCIETY AWARD

The Research Foundation Society Award is an annual award to the CFA Institute member society or societies that do the best job of using Research Foundation content in an activity, product, or service. The goal of the award is to build a strong, effective working relationship between societies and the Research Foundation.

Beginning in 2017, the award is granted to the society that has the best

- activity,
- content, or
- website design.

Some current Research Foundation programs that have evolved out of the Research Foundation Society Award include the following:

- Research Foundation content in society newsletters and on society websites
- Research Foundation author events and Research Foundation book distribution
- Research Foundation content distributed in company, university, and regulator outreach efforts
- Research Foundation content translations and creation of a book club with author conference call
- Research Foundation Research Challenge adviser presentation and Research Foundation book distribution
- Research Foundation board meeting hosting and creation of a society library with Research Foundation books

2018 Award Winners

- CFA Society New York (best website design): https://www.cfany.org/cfai-research-foundation/
- CFA Society Switzerland (best content): https://www.cfainstitute.org/en/research/foundation/2017/handbook-on-sustainable-investments
- CFA Society Brazil (best activity): http://cfasociety.org.br/

2017 Award Winners

- CFA Society Brazil (best website design)
- CFA Montréal (best content)
- CFA Society New York (best activity)

2016 Award Winners

No award issued because of a change in the timing of the Society Leaders Conference.

2015 Award Winners

- CFA Society Cleveland
- CFA Society Finland
- CFA Society France
- CFA Society Los Angeles
- CFA Society Milwaukee
- CFA Society Pakistan
- CFA Society Sydney

2014 Award Winners

- CFA China
- CFA Society San Francisco
- Indian Association of Investment Professionals
- CFA Society Philadelphia (Encouragement Award[4])

2013 Award Winners

- CFA Society Barbados
- CFA Society Hawaii
- CFA Society Pakistan
- CFA Society Italy
- CFA Society Emirates
- CFA Society Toronto
- CFA Society France (Encouragement Award)

2012 Award Winners

- Boston Security Analysts Society
- CFA Society Argentina & Uruguay
- CFA Society Buffalo
- CFA Society Bulgaria
- CFA Society Rochester
- CFA Society Seattle

The Research Foundation also extends a special thanks to societies that have hosted, or will be hosting, our trustee board meetings:

- CFA Society Toronto (Spring 2013)
- CFA Society San Francisco (Fall 2013)
- CFA Society Los Angeles (Spring 2014)
- CFA Society Minnesota (Spring 2015)
- New York Society of Security Analysts (Fall 2015)
- CFA Society Dallas/Fort Worth (Spring 2016)
- CFA Montréal (Fall 2016)
- CFA Society United Kingdom (Spring 2017)
- CFA Society Washington, DC (Fall 2017)
- CFA Society Mexico (Spring 2018)
- CFA Society Philadelphia (Fall 2018)

[4]The Encouragement Award is granted to a society whose efforts with the Research Foundation are commendable but not quite extensive enough to receive the Society Award.

RESEARCH FOUNDATION LEADERSHIP CIRCLE

The Research Foundation Leadership Circle honors investment professionals whose outstanding commitment and contributions have benefited the Research Foundation over an extended period of time. The Research Foundation is honored to recognize the following members of the Leadership Circle:

Gary Brinson, CFA

George Noyes, CFA

Frank Reilly, CFA

Fred Speece, CFA

Walter Stern, CFA

James R. Vertin, CFA

IN MEMORIAM: JAMES R. VERTIN, CFA

We are saddened to report the passing of James R. Vertin, CFA, a long-time contributor and volunteer at CFA Institute and the CFA Institute Research Foundation.

Jim was a dedicated CFA Institute volunteer and gave a significant amount of his time to our organization over the years. In fact, in recognition of all his efforts, in 1996 the CFA Institute Research Foundation established the James R. Vertin Award in his honor.

Jim's vast contributions to the organization include the following:

- ICFA board chair 1981–1982 (Institute of Chartered Financial Analysts is a predecessor organization to CFA Institute)
- FAF board member (Financial Analysts Federation is a predecessor organization to CFA Institute)
- Research Foundation board chair
- Long-time CFA Program grader
- CFA Society San Francisco society president

Jim was also a recipient of many CFA Institute awards, including the following:

- Outstanding Contribution to CFA Institute Education Programs Award, 1984 (in honor of C. Stewart Sheppard)
- CFA Institute Nicholas Molodovsky Award, 1992 (this award has since been retired)
- Donald L. Tuttle Award for CFA Grading Excellence, 2001

In his professional life, he assisted in the development of the original index fund and pioneered the application of modern portfolio management as well as the use of the computer in investment management.

Although we will miss all of Jim's contributions, the Research Foundation is proud to remember his legacy through our James R. Vertin Award and to have had him on our inaugural Research Foundation Leadership Circle.

VIII. RECENT PUBLICATIONS

RECENT PUBLICATIONS FROM THE RESEARCH FOUNDATION ARCHIVE

2017

Monographs

Equity Valuation: Science, Art, or Craft? (December)

Frank J. Fabozzi, CFA, Sergio M. Focardi, and Caroline Jonas

The price at which a stock is traded in the market reflects the ability of the firm to generate cash flow and the risks associated with generating the expected future cash flows. The authors point to the limits of widely used valuation techniques. The most important of these limits is the inability to forecast cash flows and to determine the appropriate discount rate. Another important limit is the inability to determine absolute value. Widely used valuation techniques such as market multiples—the price-to-earnings ratio, firm value multiples or a use of multiple ratios, for example—capture only relative value, that is, the value of a firm's stocks related to the value of comparable firms (assuming that comparable firms can be identified).

The study underlines additional problems when it comes to valuing IPOs and private equity: Both are sensitive to the timing of the offer, suffer from information asymmetry, and are more subject to behavioral elements than is the case for shares of listed firms. In the case of IPOs in particular, the authors discuss how communication strategies and media hype play an important role in the IPO valuation/pricing process.

https://www.cfainstitute.org/en/research/foundation/2017/equity-valuation-science-art-or-craft

Handbook on Sustainable Investments: Background Information and Practical Examples for Institutional Asset Owners (December)

Swiss Sustainable Finance

A fast growing share of investors have recently widened their scope of analysis to criteria regarded as extra-financial. They are driven by different motivations. Adoption of sustainable investment strategies can be driven, on the one hand, by the sole motivation to hedge portfolios against knowable risks by expanding the conceptual framework to incorporate the latest best practice in risk management. Other investors focus rather on a long-term view and make an active bet on societal change. Recent empirical research has shown that considering sustainability factors within investment practices does not come at a cost (i.e., through a reduced opportunity set) but allows for competitive returns. Furthermore, the growing market and resulting competition in the wake of sustainable investing going mainstream has the welcome effect to compress fees for such products. Hence, staying informed about recent trends in sustainable investing is imperative no matter what the main motivation is.

https://www.cfainstitute.org/en/research/foundation/2017/handbook-on-sustainable-investments

A Primer for Investment Trustees: Understanding Investment Committee Responsibilities (October)

Jeffery V. Bailey, CFA, and Thomas M. Richards, CFA

This "primer," written as if addressed to a new investment trustee for a university, is a comprehensive discussion of investment issues relevant not only to investment trustees but also to investment professionals who work with trustees. Taking an individual step by step through the process of responsible trusteeship, it offers a solid introduction to basic investment principles.

https://www.cfainstitute.org/en/research/foundation/2017/a-primer-for-investment-trustees

Literature Reviews

"The Equity Risk Premium: A Contextual Literature Review" (November)

Laurence B. Siegel

Research into the equity risk premium, often considered the most important number in finance, falls into three broad groupings. First, researchers have measured the margin by which equity total returns have exceeded fixed-income or cash returns over long historical periods and have projected this measure of the equity risk premium into the future. Second, the dividend discount model—or a variant of it, such as an earnings discount model—is used to estimate the future return on an equity index, and the fixed-income or cash yield is then subtracted to arrive at an equity risk premium expectation or forecast. Third, academics have used macroeconomic techniques to estimate what premium investors might rationally require for taking the risk of equities. Current thinking emphasizes the second, or dividend discount, approach and projects an equity risk premium centered on 3½% to 4%.

https://www.cfainstitute.org/en/research/foundation/2017/equity-risk-premium

Briefs

"New Vistas in Risk Profiling" (August)

Greg B. Davies

Risk profiling is fraught with misunderstandings that lead to ill-advised approaches to determining suitable investment solutions for individuals. The author discusses how we should think about the crucial elements of (a) risk tolerance, (b) behavioural risk attitudes, and (c) risk capacity. He uses a simple thought experiment to examine a stripped-down investor situation and define the essential features and exact role of each of the components of an investor's overall risk profile. He examines options for eliciting and measuring risk tolerance and considers some promising avenues for future methods.

https://www.cfainstitute.org/en/research/foundation/2017/new-vistas-in-risk-profiling

"Asian Structured Products" (August)

Angel Wu and Clarke Pitts

In this paper, we examine the nature of structured products, why they are used, and by whom. We consider the size of the industry and some of its most popular products in the context of Asian capital markets. Finally, we identify a variety of risks for each of the parties involved: issuers, intermediaries, and investors.

https://www.cfainstitute.org/en/research/foundation/2017/asian-structured-products

"FinTech and RegTech in a Nutshell, and the Future in a Sandbox" (July)

Douglas W. Arner, Jànos Barberis, and Ross P. Buckley

The 2008 global financial crisis represented a pivotal moment that separated prior phases of the development of financial technology (FinTech) and regulatory technology (RegTech) from the current paradigm. Today, FinTech has entered a phase of rapid development marked by the proliferation of startups and other new entrants, such as IT and ecommerce firms that have fragmented the financial services market. This new era presents fresh challenges for regulators and highlights why the evolution of FinTech necessitates a parallel development of RegTech. In particular, regulators must develop a robust new framework that promotes innovation and market confidence, aided by the use of regulatory "sandboxes." Certain RegTech developments today are highlighting the path toward another paradigm shift, which will be marked by a reconceptualization of the nature of financial regulation.

https://www.cfainstitute.org/en/research/foundation/2017/fintech-and-regtech-in-a-nutshell-and-the-future-in-a-sandbox

"Financial Risk Tolerance: A Psychometric Review" (June)

John E. Grable

This content provides financial analysts, investment professionals, and financial planners with a review of how financial risk-tolerance tests can and should be evaluated. It begins by clarifying terms related to risk taking and is followed by a broad overview of two important measurement terms: validity and reliability. It concludes with examples for practice.

https://www.cfainstitute.org/en/research/foundation/2017/financial-risk-tolerance

"Impact of Reporting Frequency on UK Public Companies" (March)

Robert C. Pozen, Suresh Nallareddy, and Shivaram Rajgopal

Beginning in 2007, UK public companies were required to issue quarterly, rather than semiannual, financial reports. But the UK removed this quarterly reporting requirement in 2014. We studied the effects of these regulatory changes on UK public companies and found that the frequency of financial reports had no material impact on levels of corporate investment. However, mandatory quarterly reporting was associated with an increase in analyst coverage and an improvement in the accuracy of analyst earnings forecasts.

https://www.cfainstitute.org/en/research/foundation/2017/impact-of-reporting-frequency-on-uk-public-companies

2016

Monographs

Factor Investing and Asset Allocation: A Business Cycle Perspective (December)

Vasant Naik, Mukundan Devarajan, Andrew Nowobilski, Sébastien Page, CFA, and Niels Pedersen

This monograph draws heavily on the vast body of knowledge that has been built by financial economists over the last 50 years. Its goal is to show how to solve real-life portfolio allocation problems. We have found that using a broad range of models works best. Also, we prefer simple over complex models. We believe that simplicity and modularity lend substantial robustness to investment analysis. Importantly, the framework presented provides several of the "missing links" in asset allocation—for example, the links between asset classes and risk factors, between macroeconomic views and expected returns, and ultimately between quantitative and fundamental investing.

https://www.cfainstitute.org/en/research/foundation/2016/factor-investing-and-asset-allocation-a-business-cycle-perspective

Financial Market History: Reflections on the Past for Investors Today (December)

David Chambers and Elroy Dimson

Since the 2008 financial crisis, a resurgence of interest in economic and financial history has occurred among investment professionals. This book discusses some of the lessons drawn from the past that may help practitioners when thinking about their portfolios. The book's editors, David Chambers and Elroy Dimson, are the academic leaders of the Newton Centre for Endowment Asset Management at the University of Cambridge in the United Kingdom.

https://www.cfainstitute.org/en/research/foundation/2016/financial-market-history

Let's All Learn How To Fish... To Sustain Long-Term Economic Growth (May)

Michael S. Falk, CFA

Today's economic growth challenges will become greater in the future because of the world's aging population, fertility trends and current levels, and current entitlement policies. Those challenges could be overcome, however, with thoughtful public policies and a culture that fosters responsibility and appreciation. This book reconsiders what makes us "healthy, wealthy, and wise." It focuses on how we might reimagine health care, retirement, and education policies to usher in a new ERA (from Entitlement to Responsibility with Appreciation) of sustainable long-term economic growth.

https://www.cfainstitute.org/en/research/foundation/2016/lets-all-learn-how-to-fish---to-sustain-long-term-economic-growth

Literature Reviews

"Technical Analysis: Modern Perspectives" (November)

Gordon Scott, CMT, Michael Carr, CMT, and Mark Cremonie, CMT, CFA

Supply and demand are cornerstones of economics, and the interaction of these forces is believed to explain price changes in all freely traded markets. Scarcity tends to result in increased prices and abundance generally leads to lower prices. In financial markets, technical analysis provides a framework for informing investment management decisions by applying a supply and demand methodology to market prices. Technical analysts employ a disciplined, systematic approach that seeks to minimize the impact of behavioral biases and emotions that could adversely affect investment performance. Analysts employ ratio analysis, comparative analysis, and other techniques that are similar to the tools developed to analyze financial statements.

https://www.cfainstitute.org/en/research/foundation/2017/technical-analysis

Briefs

"Gender Diversity in Investment Management: New Research for Practitioners on How to Close the Gender Gap" (September)

Rebecca Fender, CFA, Renée Adams, Brad Barber, and Terrance Odean

We've completed the largest ever survey of investment management professionals on the subject of gender diversity.

https://www.cfainstitute.org/en/research/survey-reports/gender-diversity-report

"Portfolio Structuring and the Value of Forecasting" (August)

Jacques Lussier, CFA, Andrew Ang, PhD, Mark Carhart, CFA, Craig Bodenstab, CFA, Philip E. Tetlock, Warren Hatch, CFA, and David Rapach

Drawing from a CFA Montréal event, this analysis of factor investing reviews types of factors and risk premiums as well as the value of forecasting, including issues with accuracy and improving efficiency.

https://www.cfainstitute.org/en/research/foundation/2016/portfolio-structuring-and-the-value-of-forecasting

"Overcoming the Notion of a Single Reference Currency: A Currency Basket Approach" (April)

Giuseppe Ballocchi, CFA, and Hélie d'Hautefort

Wealthy families with a global footprint have liabilities and financial objectives in multiple currencies. To manage their currency risk, it is necessary to abandon the notion of a single reference currency in favor of a customized basket of currencies. We introduce the Global Reserve Currency Index, a useful proxy for the world currency.

https://www.cfainstitute.org/en/research/foundation/2016/overcoming-the-notion-of-a-single-reference-currency-a-currency-basket-approach

"Annuities and Retirement Income Planning" (February)

Patrick J. Collins, CFA

Annuitization is one asset management strategy for retirees seeking to secure lifetime income. The US annuity marketplace offers a variety of annuity contracts, including single premium annuities, advanced life deferred annuities, variable annuities with lifetime income guarantee riders, and ruin contingent deferred annuities. Advisers seeking to provide guidance to clients in or near retirement can benefit by understanding (1) the arguments both for and against annuitization and (2) how a client's interests might be best represented in the marketplace. Important annuity contract provisions are highlighted and briefly discussed so the adviser can become more familiar with retirement-planning options.

https://www.cfainstitute.org/en/research/foundation/2016/annuities-and-retirement-income-planning

"Risk Profiling through a Behavioral Finance Lens" (February)

Michael Pompian, CFA

This piece examines risk profiling through a behavioral finance lens. Advisers can classify clients into behavioral investor types to help determine what kind of investment plan they should recommend. With a better understanding of behavioral finance vis-à-vis risk taking, practitioners can enhance their understanding of client preferences and better inform their recommendations of investment strategies and products.

https://www.cfainstitute.org/en/research/foundation/2016/risk-profiling-through-a-behavioral-finance-lens

2015

Monographs

The Industrial Organization of the Global Asset Management Business (November)

Ingo Walter

The dynamics of the asset management business are complex and geographically diverse. Products and vendors compete within and across markets and often shade into each other. Regulation can differ dramatically according to financial systems and functions. Here are discussed the major asset management sectors—pension funds, mutual funds, alternative investment vehicles, and private wealth management. Despite the complexity of the industry, common threads run through the discussion—growth, risk, and cost—that cannot be ignored by asset managers hoping to be sustainably profitable. What is required to excel includes distribution in leading markets, product breadth and consistency, global money management expertise, and capital strength. Also needed are technological capability, marketing and customer service skills, defensible pricing, low-cost production, and a strong brand. All these characteristics must be rooted in an affirmative culture with cohesive senior management and a talented and motivated staff.

https://www.cfainstitute.org/en/research/foundation/2015/the-industrial-organization-of-the-global-asset-management-business

Trading and Electronic Markets: What Investment Professionals Need to Know (October)

Larry Harris, CFA

The true meaning of investment discipline is to trade only when you rationally expect that you will achieve your desired objective. Accordingly, managers must thoroughly understand why they trade. Because trading is a zero-sum game, good investment discipline also requires that managers understand why their counterparties trade. This book surveys the many reasons why people trade and identifies the implications of the zero-sum game for investment discipline. It also identifies the origins of liquidity and thus of transaction costs, as well as when active investment strategies are profitable. The book then explains how managers must measure and control transaction costs to perform well. Electronic trading systems and electronic trading strategies now dominate trading in exchange markets throughout the world. The book identifies why speed is of such great importance to electronic traders, how they obtain it, and the trading strategies they use to exploit it. Finally, the book analyzes many issues associated with electronic trading that currently concern practitioners and regulators.

https://www.cfainstitute.org/en/research/foundation/2015/trading-and-electronic-markets-what-investment-professionals-need-to-know

A Comprehensive Guide to Exchange-Traded Funds (ETFs) (May)

Joanne M. Hill, Dave Nadig, and Matt Hougan

Exchange-traded funds (ETFs) have become in their 25-year history one of the fastest growing segments of the investment management business. These funds provide liquid access to virtually every financial market and allow large and small investors to build institutional-caliber portfolios. Yet, their management fees are significantly lower than those typical of mutual funds. High levels of transparency in ETFs for holdings and investment strategy help investors evaluate an ETF's potential returns and risks. This book covers the evolution of ETFs as products and in their uses in investment strategies. It details how ETFs work, their unique investment and trading features, their regulatory structure, how they are used in tactical and strategic portfolio management in a broad range of asset classes, and how to evaluate them individually.

https://www.cfainstitute.org/en/research/foundation/2015/a-comprehensive-guide-to-exchange-traded-funds-etfs

Literature Reviews

"Longevity Risk and Retirement Income Planning" (November)

Patrick J. Collins, CFA, Huy D. Lam, CFA, and Josh Stampfli

The past 50 years have seen an abundance of research on retirement planning and longevity risk. Reviewed here is the academic side of the research and its varied viewpoints and nuances. The evolution of retirement risk models, retirement portfolio problems and solutions, and annuities are some of the many topics covered.

https://www.cfainstitute.org/en/research/foundation/2015/longevity-risk-and-retirement-income-planning

Briefs

"Investor Risk Profiling: An Overview" (April)

Joachim Klement, CFA

The current standard process of risk profiling through questionnaires is highly unreliable and typically explains less than 15% of the variation in risky assets between investors—mostly because the questionnaires focus on socio-economic variables and hypothetical scenarios. The existing research in risk profiling shows, however, that several factors can provide more accurate and reliable insights into the risk profile of investors. Among these factors are the lifetime experiences an investor has had, the financial decisions made in the past, and the influence of family and friends as well as advisers. By using these factors, practitioners can get a better understanding of their clients' preferences in order to recommend suitable investment strategies and products.

https://www.cfainstitute.org/en/research/foundation/2015/investor-risk-profiling-an-overview

Made in the USA
Las Vegas, NV
08 November 2026

57691397R00057